What's the
DIFFERENCE?

How to Tell Things Apart
That Are Confusingly Close

MARC TYLER NOBLEMAN

BARNES & NOBLE
NEW YORK

The difference between the almost right word and the right word is really a large matter—'tis the difference between the lightning-bug and the lightning.

—*Mark Twain*

A BARNES & NOBLE BOOK

Copyright © 2005 by Quirk Packaging, Inc.
Text copyright © 2005 by Marc Tyler Nobleman
Cover illustrations © 2005 by John Stislow

A Quirk Packaging Book
Designed by Lynne Yeamans and Stephanie Stislow
Edited by Sarah Scheffel and Liana Krissoff

ISBN: 0-7607-7493-5

Printed & bound in the United States of America

10 9 8 7 6 5 4 3 2 1

What's the difference?

CONTENTS

What's the difference between...
a PREFACE, an INTRODUCTION, and a FOREWORD?

All you know is that they're at the front of the book and you skip over them.

A **preface** is a short discussion by the author about the aim, background, or structure of the book. It can come before the contents page, though it doesn't always, and introductions and forewords rarely if ever do. If the author's acknowledgments aren't extensive, they're sometimes collapsed into the preface. (Mine are on the next page.)

An **introduction** is an often lengthy discussion by the author about the subject of the book. It can serve a purpose similar to a movie preview—to lure the reader to the main attraction. The introduction is frequently part of the text proper, and, if so, it inaugurates the Arabic-numeral page numbering (as opposed to the lowercase Roman numerals often used for other front matter).

A **foreword** is a discussion of the book by someone other than the author. It is framed in terms of the subject of the book, the reason(s) the author wrote the book, the reason(s) a reader should check out the book, or a combination thereof. Publishers try to score a foreword written by a high-profile person and then highlight his or her name on the cover to help sell the book (maybe even in a larger font than the author's name).

*   *   *   *   *

To make it into this book, a comparison had to be one of two types:
1. a pair or group that people commonly confuse (such as alligator and crocodile; see page 8); or
2. a pair or group that people don't commonly confuse yet can't articulate the difference between (such as fruit and vegetable, see page 50).

I've avoided differences between pairs and groups that are merely synonyms—let's leave that to the "commonly confused words" lists in nearly every style and usage guide. However, since I already gave my "exceptions" disclaimer, here's the first—there are a few entries that do turn out to be about synonyms, but synonyms with substance; their story is in how people assume they're different.

And of course, there are countless other titillating comparisons that didn't fit in this book but that may be in future editions. To that end, please send any suggestions or comments about this book to difference@quirkpackaging.com.

Marc Tyler Nobleman
May 30, 2005 (Memorial Day; see page 64)

Acknowledgments

Thanks to Sharyn Rosart at Quirk Packaging, who gave my pitch a chance and got it in front of the receptive minds of the people at Barnes & Noble, and to Sarah Scheffel at QP, who edited with patience and perception. I recognize all you did to make this book happen. Thanks to the throng of friends too numerous to name who responded to my e-mail survey with the distinctions they're unclear on. I've done e-mail surveys for projects before, but none prompted as high a response rate as this one, which I took as a good sign that this topic would have an eager audience. Most of all, thank you to Daniela, who in supporting my writing schedule was temporarily reminded of the difference between a husband and a virtual stranger.

What's the difference?

ANIMALS

What's the difference between...
an ALLIGATOR and a CROCODILE?

Unscientific research suggests that this may be *the* most classic "what's the difference" question. A superficial answer is that alligators are abbreviated at the tail end ("gator") and crocodiles at the snout ("croc"). As for the other differences, for the love of bogs, don't get close enough to find out for yourself. It's infinitely safer to keep reading instead.

ALLIGATOR

An alligator is a reptile (see page 22) of the family **Alligatoridae.** (In case animal classification is as foggy a grade-school memory as the Dewey Decimal System, here's a refresher: kingdom, phylum, class, order, family, genus, species.)

Generally, alligators are characterized by **broad, U-shaped snouts,** though, as with most animal distinctions, there are exceptions. Their upper jaw overlaps their lower jaw. When their jaws are closed, the upper teeth are visible and the lower teeth are hidden—even the large fourth lower tooth on both sides.

CROCODILE

The crocodile is a reptile of the family **Crocodylidae.**

In general, their snouts are **narrow and V-shaped.** The upper and lower jaws of crocodiles are roughly the same width, and both upper and lower teeth jut out when their mouths are closed. The fourth lower tooth of each side sticks out prominently. (We get it—you're menacing.)

Crocodiles have developed a reputation for being the more aggressive crocodilian (a collective term for both animals), but that doesn't mean you can cuddle with an alligator with any more security.

The salt glands on their tongues are essentially inactive, so alligators are usually **restricted to fresh water.** The black spots on alligator jaws are sensory organs called dermal pressure receptors (DPRs). They help the reptiles adjust to changes in water pressure.

Alligators are found only in the **southeastern United States and China.** They range in coloration from gray to black and on average reach a length of **fifteen feet** (4.6 m).

The salt glands on crocodile tongues secrete excess salt from the body, which gives crocodiles a **high tolerance for salt water.** Crocodiles also have DPRs, but all over their bodies, not just on their heads.

Crocodiles live in **various warm regions** around the world. The only place they're found in the United States—and the only known place where they share a habitat with alligators—is in southern Florida. They're typically a tan or brown color and can grow to **eighteen feet** (5.5 m), and occasionally longer.

What's the difference between...
a DOLPHIN and a PORPOISE?

Even though dolphins and porpoises can't do long division (or so we think), both may be almost as smart as you. When asked what distinguishes them from each other, however, neither seems able to articulate it—or maybe those squeaks are answers, and we're just too dumb to understand them. Here is what we simple-minded humans have figured out about these aquatic acrobats.

DOLPHIN

Dolphins have pointy, **cone-shaped teeth,** and many types of dolphins have what looks like a beak, actually called a *rostrum.* They are bigger than porpoises—they can be more than **ten feet (3 m) long.**

Though not all dolphins have dorsal (back) fins, pay attention to the appearance of those that do. Typically, a dolphin's **dorsal fin is hooked,** like a wave.

PORPOISE

Porpoises have **spade-shaped teeth,** and their snouts are less beaklike than dolphins'. While they tend to look plumper than dolphins, they're smaller—usually no more than **seven feet (2.1 m) long.**

A porpoise's dorsal fin, if it has one, is triangular, **reminiscent of a shark fin.**

The oceans are home to more than thirty species of dolphin and six species of porpoise. Despite their majority, dolphins give no indication of a superiority complex.

Dolphins produce sounds that humans can hear.

You're likelier to catch sight of a dolphin in the wild than a porpoise. If a **sleek, friendly mammal** is racing your boat, chances are it's a dolphin. Those performers at water theme parks are probably dolphins, too.

Porpoises emit sounds at a frequency our ears are not sensitive enough to pick up.

Porpoises, which live in colder water than dolphins do, on the whole are **less frequently spotted by humans.** Maybe they're just off practicing their long division.

RELATED TERMS: *Both dolphins and porpoises are* **mammals.** *More specifically, both are types of* **whales.** *One of the largest types of dolphins is the killer whale. Kind of like finding out your puppy is related to a werewolf (see page 110), huh?*

What's the difference between...
a FROG and a TOAD?

Frogs and toads are both tailless amphibians (see page 22) of the order Anura that have been assigned to separate families. However, some animals qualify as both frog and toad, as expert frogologists and toadaphiles will be quick to point out.

FROG	TOAD
Frogs (in the family Ranidae, the "true frogs") generally have **smooth, moist skin,** longer hind legs for swimming and leaping, and webbed hind feet. They're usually slender compared to toads.	Toads (in the family Bufonidae, the "true toads") generally have **warty, dry skin** and shorter hind legs—for walking rather than marathon hopping. They're typically stout compared to frogs.
Frogs insist on **waterfront** property and don't venture far from it like toads might.	Toads are more **terrestrial,** though like good amphibians, they breed in water.
Frog eggs are clumped in a **cloudy, jellylike mass.**	Toads' **eggs are stringy chains** that snake around aquatic plants. A few types of toads bear live young. Don't make a toad angry. If it's one of several types, you may trigger the two glands near its head that ooze poison.

Whether you call it a frog or a toad often comes down to how it looks. Of course, another major difference is that frogs get more coverage in fairy tales (see page 106).

Flying Fish / Flying Squirrel / Flying Fox

Judging by our planes, hang gliders, and jet packs, we humans have a serious bird complex. So do some other animals–but they don't rely on machines to get their fix. They just get up there and do it. (Makes us look pretty lazy, huh?)

At one time or another, most of us have been red-faced when we couldn't identify which of these three types of flying non-birds just buzzed us. Yet the way they fly is the way they differ. A flying fish uses its fins to jump and soar. A flying squirrel uses flaps of skin on the side of its body between its forelegs and hind legs. A flying fox uses wings, like a bat–because that's what it really is. You didn't really think a fox could fly, did you?

What's the difference between…
a GERBIL and a HAMSTER?

These critters do exist beyond the cages of many a child's room, but the following distinctions address them exclusively as pets.

GERBIL

A gerbil is a classification of rodent native to desert regions of Africa and Asia. The Mongolian gerbil is the species most commonly seen as a pet. Gerbils are now bred in **multiple colors,** though hot pink is not yet available.

Gerbils have long hind feet and **long, furry, tufted tails.** A pet gerbil is typically smaller than your basic golden hamster.

HAMSTER

A hamster is a classification of rodent native to Europe and Asia. The most popular pet breed is the golden hamster, sometimes called the Syrian hamster. You'd think the fur coloring of a golden hamster is a no-brainer, but they're actually closer to **reddish brown or even gray.**

Hamsters' **tails are stubby and bare.** Known for their expandable cheek pouches, hamsters sometimes store food there, then bury it in their cage shavings, then dig it back up and eat it.

Though gerbils are primarily nocturnal, they can also be **found awake during the day**—well, in between naps. On average, they live four to five years.

Gerbils are **sociable** little fuzzballs, both with humans and with their own kind. They can be kept in single-sex pairs and may even get depressed if they're not. Gerbils are gentle and rarely bite, though that doesn't mean you want to let them roam free through your house. They can be excitable, and sometimes slap their hind legs on the ground when they're about to be fed. As long as their environment is kept clean, gerbils are generally **odor-free.**

Like gerbils, hamsters are nocturnal, but they're **rarely active during the day.** In fact, if you awaken them to play, they may nip. The average hamster life span is two to three years, which, though it may seem short to us, is a long time to be confined to a small, boring cage.

Hamsters are **solitary** by nature and usually need to be kept alone, as they tend to fight with and can even kill their supposed compatriots. They may even resist bonding with their owners. This may be a welcome trait, as hamsters have a tendency to **stink.**

a HAWK and a FALCON?

These birds hunt for small mammals or lizards with their beaks and talons, which makes them both raptors that belong to the order Falconiformes. They're commonly confused, though the differences become most clear when you see them from the perspective of their prey.

HAWK

A hawk is a member of the family Accipitridae, which also includes eagles. "True hawks" are also called accipiters. The word *hawk* is sometimes used to refer to a bird of prey in general. Compared to falcon wings, **hawk wings are short and broad** and have more rounded tips.

Hawks fly in a **flap-soar pattern,** meaning they move their wings several times, then glide for a period. To capture live prey, they fly at low altitudes, pursuing it as it scurries across the ground.

FALCON

The falcon is a member of the family Falconidae. Falcon **wings are longer and more pointed** than hawk wings.

Falcons are fast, almost **frenzied fliers.** They catch live prey by stooping, or swooping down rapidly. "True falcons" are known for their notched beaks, giving them what can look like a tooth.

Most hawks **build nests** from twigs in trees.

Because hawks tend to be less keen on human companionship than falcons are, they're not used as much in sport—hence falconry, not hawkry. When hawks are used for hunting, they are typically sent after small land animals, notably rabbits.

Instead of building their own nests, falcons save time by **moving into abandoned nests** of other birds, or just laying eggs on a cliff ledge or even on the ground.

Falcons can be trained to capture game, especially other birds, on cue. The popularity of falconry peaked among European nobles during the Middle Ages, but it's still a pastime today. If you fantasize about wearing huge gloves (and don't fear notched beaks), falconry may be right for you.

What's the difference between...
a MONKEY, an APE, and a CHIMPANZEE?

Here's a start: a chimp is not a monkey but an ape. Here's a tangent: you are pretty much an ape, too. And finally, a fact that may alarm even the most open-minded evolutionists—biologically, chimps are closer to humans than they are to gorillas.

MONKEY

A monkey is a **primate—and not a type of ape.** Monkeys come in many varieties, including baboons, mandrills, marmosets, capuchins, spider monkeys, and howler monkeys, but one feature nearly all exhibit is a **tail.** Some of those tails are prehensile (adapted for seizing or grasping), others aren't. Monkeys are more similar to other mammals than apes are, and they're generally smaller than apes. Contrary to simian lore, monkeys do not swing through the jungle on vines. Instead, they scuttle through the trees along branches. On the ground, they move on all fours, soles down and palms raised. Monkeys can be found on **four continents** (tough luck, North America, Australia, and Antarctica).

APE

An ape is a **primate—and not a type of monkey.** Examples of apes are gorillas, orangutans, bonobos, and chimpanzees. In fact, those four constitute the "great apes," the most mentally complex known creatures on Earth short of humans, if you consider low-carb brownies and pop-up ads to be products of a genius species. Gibbons are also apes, just not "great" ones. Apes **don't have external tails,** though their coccyx bone is the remnant of a tail that got lost along the evolutionary trail. They travel through trees by hanging from branches and advancing arm-over-arm. Apes have the capability of upright posture for varying lengths of time, though their locomotion is on all fours with the digits on their forelimbs tucked under their knuckles. They live in **Africa and Asia.**

CHIMPANZEE

A chimpanzee is a **type of ape,** which means it's a primate but not a monkey. Chimps are available in two species: the common chimp and the bonobo, sometimes called the pygmy chimpanzee. Like humans, chimps use simple tools. (In fairness, some monkeys do too, but chimps seem to be more advanced in this department.) The only continent on which wild chimps live is **Africa.**

Though some object to classifying humans as apes, humans and great apes do fall into the same family, Hominidae. Humans even share a subfamily with gorillas and chimps, Homininae.

What's the difference between...
a PANTHER, a LEOPARD, and a JAGUAR?

Lions and tigers and bears, nobody mixes up. (Bears: What are they doing in this bunch, anyway?) But the distinctions among the B-list big cats tend to blur like cheetah spots at top speed.

PANTHER

The term *panther* has two meanings. One, a panther is a big cat of the genus *Panthera*. This comprises the four that are capable of roaring: lions, tigers, leopards, and jaguars. Two, a panther (or black panther) is a big cat born with dark fur due to a high concentration of the skin pigment melanin. In other words, a panther is **not a species but a coloring variant.** For example, both leopards and jaguars can be panthers. And upon close examination or in the right angle of sunlight, you'd see that panthers still have their dark spots—only they blend in with the dark rest of them.

LEOPARD

A leopard is a spotted big cat. Wild leopards are found exclusively in **Africa and Asia.** Leopard spots are typically small, circular, and filled in. They're spattered closely together on the fur in a **consistent pattern.** Leopards are leaner and smaller than jaguars. They also have more compact heads and longer tails.

Leopards rely on their tails to help them keep their balance in trees, where they often go to escape even larger predators like lions or to feast on a kill without being disturbed by scavengers. The maximum size of an adult leopard is around **120 pounds** (54 kg).

JAGUAR

A jaguar is also a spotted big cat, but on the other side of the Atlantic. Wild jaguars are found only in **Central and South America.** Jaguar **markings vary on different parts of the body**—small, solid spots on the neck and shoulders, large, solid spots on the legs, and large, splotchy rings on the flank and back. The rings are called rosettes, and frequently have one or several dark spots inside them. Compared to leopards, jaguars are larger with a broader head and stockier legs. Jaguar tails are shorter than leopard tails. No other animal in the jaguar's native habitat is powerful enough to challenge one over a kill, so jaguars usually don't need to—though they can—climb trees. Adult jaguars can weigh up to **300 pounds** (136 kg), which makes them almost twice as heavy as leopards.

RELATED TERMS: *A* **cheetah** *is a spotted big cat of Africa and the world's fastest known land animal. The cheetah's small spots are solid, not ringed. Cheetahs have smaller heads and more svelte legs than leopards or jaguars, and they're leaner. The range of the cheetah overlaps with that of the leopard.*

A **puma** *is a big, uniformly tawny cat that lives throughout the Americas. Along with jaguars, pumas are the only wild big cats in the Western Hemisphere.* **Cougar** *and* **mountain lion** *are among the regional terms for puma. In the United States, pumas are sometimes called* panthers, *whether they're black or not.*

What's the difference between...
a REPTILE and an AMPHIBIAN?

At different times in the distant past, both the reptiles and the amphibians were the dominant animals on Earth. How the slithery and slimy have fallen; now the average person can't tell them apart. And no, the difference between the two has nothing to do with whether they live on land or in water—some reptiles live in the water and some amphibians live on land. Rather, they are primarily distinguished in two key ways: skin and eggs.

REPTILE

A reptile has **dry, scaly skin**, and most have clawed feet. Reptiles **have lungs** and can't breathe through their skin, though they can shed it.

A **reptile roll call** includes alligators and crocodiles (see page 8), lizards, snakes, tortoises, and turtles.

AMPHIBIAN

An amphibian has **moist skin** and often webbed feet—but never clawed feet. The skin of amphibians can be smooth or bumpy, but it **must stay wet** in order for them to stay hydrated and to breathe. Yes, they "drink" and absorb oxygen through their skin, though some amphibians also have lungs.

Taking attendance of amphibians, there are frogs and toads (see page 12), newts, salamanders, and a group called caecilians. None of them have scales—or, for that matter, any other skin covering, such as hair. Some types of amphibians have skin that is toxic to the touch, a trait not found in reptiles.

About the only thing you might remember from grade school about reptiles and amphibians is that they're cold-blooded, meaning they can't generate their own body heat and must get it from their environment. "Cold-blooded" is misleading, however. Better to say these animals are ectotherms.

Some reptiles, such as alligators and crocodiles, spend time in water, but not all do, and most lay their eggs on land. Even marine reptiles such as turtles hit the shore to have babies. Reptile **eggs are hard-shelled and amniotic.** A few types of reptiles don't lay their eggs—but technically they don't give birth to live young, either. The babies are in eggs that remain within their mothers' bodies, and they come out of both the egg and the mother at the same time. Like baby humans, baby reptiles resemble **miniature versions of their parents,** though sometimes their coloring may differ.

All amphibians lay eggs—but none do that reptile trick of keeping them inside till birth. Their **eggs are soft and jellylike** and must be in or near water to hatch. Baby amphibians **don't look like their parents** but rather like fish, complete with gills— they're fully aquatic at first. Through metamorphosis, these larvae (or tadpoles) will eventually lose their tails and sprout legs, then check out land.

What's the difference?

PEOPLE

DANIEL BOONE and DAVY CROCKETT

DWARF and MIDGET

GEEK and NERD

HOBO, TRAMP, and BUM

OPTICIAN, OPTOMETRIST, and OPHTHALMOLOGIST

PILGRIM and PURITAN

PIRATE, CORSAIR, PRIVATEER, and BUCCANEER

What's the difference between...
DANIEL BOONE and DAVY CROCKETT?

You might think this entry is a joke, yet when pressed, you probably can't name one fact about each of these men. You feel like one (or was it both?) wore a coonskin cap. Maybe one was at the Alamo? See...you're stumped. They *are* easily confused. So hitch up the wagon and load the rifle. We're heading to the frontier South.

DANIEL BOONE

Daniel Boone (1734–1820) was an American explorer and a **central figure in the settlement of Kentucky.** Born in Pennsylvania, his family later moved to North Carolina, where Boone proved to be a skilled hunter. Beginning in 1767, he began to explore the region surrounding the Kentucky River, which was still unknown to white settlers. He blazed a trail to Kentucky that was named the **Wilderness Road.** Once there, he founded the village of Boonesboro (or Boonesborough) in 1775.

(Okay, it's no Chicago, but what villages have *you* founded?) Boone served in the Virginia militia as well as the Virginia legislature, as Kentucky was part of Virginia at the time. In between all this, he found time to fight both Indians and the British during the American Revolution. He ended up in Missouri, where he died at his home, already a legend (see page 107). Call Boone a pioneer, a patriot, or a folk hero. Just don't call him Danny (or Davy).

Besides their beloved status, is anything else the same about these guys? Though both have been famously depicted with coonskin caps, neither wore them in real life.

DAVY CROCKETT

Davy Crockett (1786–1836) was an **American backwoodsman** who became a U.S. representative and died at the Alamo. (Boone was fifty-two when Crockett was born. In other words, they didn't exactly hang out.) Born in Tennessee, Crockett became a member of the state (see page 68) legislature and was then **elected to Congress,** where he served from 1827 to 1831 and from 1833 to 1835. When Crockett left public office, he did something you don't see former government types today doing: he went to war. Texas was then a part of Mexico, but wanted out. Crockett joined their efforts to secede. In 1836, from inside a San Antonio mission called the Alamo, he and fewer than two hundred rebels fought off an estimated sixteen hundred Mexican soldiers. Crockett and most of the rest of the Americans were **killed at the Alamo,** but Texas won its independence only a few weeks later. Call Crockett a politician, a martyr, or king of the wild frontier. Just don't call him David (or Daniel).

What's the difference between...
a DWARF and a MIDGET?

Within most circles, *dwarf* is an acceptable term for a person of shorter than average height as a result of genetics. *Midget* is nearly always considered derogatory. Other prevailing terms include *little person* or *person of short stature*.

DWARF

A dwarf is a person who has a genetic or metabolic condition of **stunted growth** and who is therefore **disproportionate** in some way—disproportionate only as compared to a person without dwarfism. According to the organization the Little People of America, an adult dwarf can reach a height of **four feet, ten inches** (147 cm), or possibly a bit taller.

Dwarfism is sometimes referred to by the name of any of the specific forms this condition can take, such as **achondroplasia.** A person with achondroplasia—the most common of the approximately 200 types of dwarfism—has a trunk of average size but short limbs and sometimes a head of above average size.

MIDGET

Formerly, *midget* sometimes referred to a person who was **considerably below average height** but who had the **proportions of a person of average height.** Today, regardless of proportions, a person who is below average height due to a medical condition is properly called a dwarf.

RELATED TERM: *A* **pygmy** *(sometimes capitalized) is an anthropological, not scientific, term for a person under five feet (152 cm) tall, particularly a member of certain groups living in central Africa. They are not considered dwarfs.*

No medical treatment is available (or necessary, according to most), though some little people elect to undergo controversial "limb-lengthening" surgery.

Aside from experiencing certain inconveniences, most people with dwarfism are capable of living their lives as anyone else would. Their intelligence is unaffected. By the way, you're a bit early for the "myth" section of this book, so don't use the plural form *dwarves* here—that refers only to the little people of fantasy. The plural in the real world is *dwarfs.*

Because this condition is often a sign of a hormonal deficiency, it can be **treated medically.**

The negative connotation of the word *midget* can be traced to the mid-1800s, when little people were put on display in carnival freak shows. While *midget* has fallen out of favor when used to refer to humans, it is still used as a classification for other things, such as racing cars.

What's the difference between...
a GEEK and a NERD?

If you're a school-aged bully, you probably don't care—either one is fodder for mocking. If you're in the adult world, you probably use the words interchangeably as well, most likely in reference to your boss or your brother-in-law or both. Take note, Judgmental One: this kind of labeling does a disservice to both species. It surely will not be surprising to learn that the Internet is brimming with message board posts debating this subject. Equally unsurprising, consensus is elusive.

A geek seems to be **any smart person with an obsessive interest.** Despite widespread misconception, that interest does not have to be computers or *Star Trek*. While those are two of the most visible kinds of geeks, there are also comic book geeks, reality TV geeks, World War II geeks, motorcycle geeks, organic food geeks, politics geeks, and even sports geeks. As such, **most of us are geeks** of one kind or another, whether or not we admit it. Yes, geeks are more mainstream than previously believed. If you've got a passion and a serviceable IQ, you're living proof. Geeks like to talk about the object of their affection, sometimes far more than anyone is willing to listen.

A nerd is any smart person with an obsessive interest, but also a **lack of social grace.** (Yes, this implies that geeks can indeed have social grace.) Nerds are uncompromisingly pure, often more comfortable with themselves than non-nerds are. They are not by definition wimpy. In fact, they are courageous because they do not give in to the expectations of a superficial society. The one possible exception to this is their drive to excel academically, particularly in the realm of intelligence testing: nerds are promiscuous studiers. It's a generalization rooted in truth that they gravitate toward math, science, and technology.

Geeks can blend in, nerds stand out, though **neither craves acceptance.** Except for a few stressful teenage years, geeks and nerds have no shame about their classification. While both words were at one time insulting, nowadays they

The word "geek" used to have a far more unappealing connotation: a carnival performer who bites the heads off live chickens or snakes. A commonly cited first appearance of "nerd" is Dr. Seuss's book *If I Ran the Zoo* (1950).

are routinely used as terms of endearment. Geeks and nerds would go so far as say they take pride in these monikers.

Geekdom is a lifestyle choice and **nerddom is quite possibly genetic,** though even a cursory check of any decade-old high school yearbook will invariably turn up a nerd who has since beaten biology and blossomed into hunkdom or babedom. Geeks interact with nongeeks, sometimes quite successfully. Nerds prefer to—or have no choice but to—hang with their own kind. Both geeks and nerds can be extroverted, but the effect is different: **geeks annoy and nerds elicit (unneeded) sympathy.**

There is less diversity among nerds than among geeks. The many geek factions do not necessarily get along, but nerds do have the potential to be a unified front. If nerds ever do choose to seek revenge (see page 88) as the 1980s movie imagines, they'd be a formidable force, with or without pocket protectors.

RELATED TERMS: *A* **dweeb** *is a nerd with an extra piece of tape around the nose bridge of his glasses—in other words, a "mega nerd." A* **dork** *is a person you don't even pretend to like, with good reason. Unlike most geeks, nerds, and dweebs, dorks are often stupid, grating, or otherwise unpleasant.*

What's the difference between...
a HOBO, a TRAMP, and a BUM?

Today, homelessness is not romanticized, but for about thirty years on either end of 1900, it was, to varying degrees. Perhaps a better term for it then would've been "houselessness." Many of the men who chose the vagabond way of life would have said that they didn't have a house but they sure had a home—the open plains, seen chugging by from the open door of a boxcar.

HOBO

A hobo was a person who **traveled and looked for work.** Sometimes, when work dried up where he lived, a man was forced to become itinerant, but often a hobo was a hobo by choice. Toting their bindles, hoboes snuck aboard the baggage cars of trains to get from place to place, but were otherwise largely honorable. They **rode the rails** in their greatest numbers from the 1870s to the 1940s, but secured a place in the pantheon of American cultural archetypes during the height of homelessness, the Great Depression. They accepted jobs at farms, construction sites, mills, mines, shops, even private homes. A brotherhood sprung up around these transient laborers. They began as a bunch of strangers traveling alone, but they had the same purpose, embraced the uncertainty of their situation in the same spirit, and frequently headed in the same direction. The **lifestyle was risky,** but for many hoboes, the independence was worth the dangers. Hoboes and the freedom associated with their pick-up-and-go lifestyle served as inspiration to the Beat Generation of the 1950s and the hippie counterculture of the 1960s.

At the time, those on the streets (see page 139) summarized their differences along these lines: a hobo wandered and worked, a tramp wandered and dreamed, a bum stayed still and drank.

TRAMP

A tramp was a person who **traveled but didn't look for work.** While tramps may have picked up the occasional temporary job, they got by mostly by begging or scavenging. Rather than hop on freight trains, they tended to move around **on foot.** Some hitchhiked. The term *tramp* found a place in the parlance soon after the American Civil War, a few decades before *hobo* did in the 1890s.

BUM

A bum was a person who **didn't travel,** didn't work or look for work, and **subsisted by begging or stealing.** Hoboes and probably tramps did not respect bums, and hoboes in particular disliked being mistaken for them. The label of "bum" post-dated "hobo," coming into general use in the 1940s. Now *bum* is a derogatory term used to describe a homeless person, whereas *hobo* and *tramp* are seldom heard.

What's the difference between...
an OPTICIAN, an OPTOMETRIST, and an OPHTHALMOLOGIST?

The obvious answer is that the first two are easy to spell and the last is borderline maddening. Or perhaps that's just in the eye of the beholder. Regardless, here's a more practical answer that distinguishes between the beholders of the eye.

OPTICIAN

An optician is a professional able to fulfill prescriptions for corrective eyewear. That includes **preparing and adjusting glasses.** (Additional training is necessary to dispense contact lenses.) Opticians receive **two years of training** at an accredited technical school. They are **not doctors.**

OPTOMETRIST

An optometrist (O.D., a doctor of optometry) is a practitioner charged with conducting **eye exams,** which can include fitting for contact lenses and diagnosing infections and disorders. Optometrists earn a bachelor of science degree followed by a **four-year optometry degree.** This education includes eye anatomy and physiology. Like opticians, optometrists are **not medical doctors,** but optometrists can handle pre- and postoperative care and prescribe treatment. In other words, optometrists can do whatever an optician can do, and then some.

OPHTHALMOLOGIST

An ophthalmologist (M.D. or D.O., a doctor of osteopathy) is a **medical doctor** who may perform **eye surgery.** Ophthalmologists take into account the relationship between the eyes and the rest of the body, since conditions such as diabetes and multiple sclerosis can affect the eyes, too. Ophthalmologists complete at least **twelve years of school,** comprising college (see page 60), medical school, and residency. In general, ophthalmologists are capable of doing anything optometrists can do.

What's the difference between...
a PILGRIM and a PURITAN?

If you're already dreading Thanksgiving because of the same old family patterns, whether it's continuous bickering or tedious gossiping, salvation is upon you. The answer to this question will change not only the table conversation but your childhood perception of the first colonists to leave England (see page 132) and come to what is now Massachusetts.

In 1620, a mere 102 people—the ones we've come to know as Pilgrims—sailed the *Mayflower* to Plymouth. Some were **Puritans, members of a division of Protestantism** who believed that the Church of England was corrupt and wanted to "purify" it rather than abandon it. But when they decided the Church was beyond reform, they'd split from it—then split England altogether to escape persecution.

RELATED TERMS: *Other labels for those first Europeans to relocate to New England are bandied about. Since the 1945 publication of a book called* Saints and Strangers, *by George Willison, some historians use* **"Saints"** *to describe the Plymouth colonists, but the colonists didn't. To a seventeenth-century Englishman, a saint was a member of God's chosen people, not specifically the Plymouth folks. (However, William Bradford did mention the word in the same manuscript in which he used "Pilgrim.") In his chronicle of Plymouth, Bradford called the Plymouth colonists* **"strangers."** *He meant the word the way we do today—people we don't know—but, like "saint," it wasn't commonly used as a group title.*

Pilgrims, Puritans, Separatists, Saints, strangers...if it's still confusing, maybe you'll want to stick to the Thanksgiving bickering after all.

According to their own letters and other documents, these religious dissidents did not call themselves Puritans *or* Pilgrims. In fact, there was no one term for them during their own era. At various times, they referred to themselves as Planters, Old Comers, or Forefathers. But a term that church loyalists disparagingly called them gained more currency: **Separatists.**

Of those 102 *Mayflower* passengers, only 41 were Separatists. The other 61 were non-Separatists heading to America not for religious freedom but for economic opportunity (although many joined the Separatists' church after arrival).

The word *pilgrim* **(lowercase *p*) means "homeless wanderer"** and often has a religious connotation. In that sense, the 1620 bunch were pilgrims, but they didn't come to be known as Pilgrims (capital *p*) until after the 1820 Plymouth bicentennial. During that celebration, a single passage referencing "Pilgrim Fathers" from a manuscript by early Plymouth governor William Bradford was popularized—and eventually immortalized.

A substantially larger wave of English people came to the Massachusetts Bay in 1630 and founded Boston. They were mostly non-Separatist Puritans who left England in hopes of improving their economic prospects.

What's the difference between...
a PIRATE, a CORSAIR, a PRIVATEER, and a BUCCANEER?

On the high seas in the golden age of piracy (roughly 1680 to 1725), when a band of ruffians boarded a ship to plunder, they didn't flash a badge to indicate what type of criminals they were.

PIRATE

A pirate was a sea-based outlaw who **robbed without authorization from any nation**—it was for personal gain. All ships and ports were fair targets for pirates. They had a reputation for viciousness and even fearlessness.

Pirates still exist today with much the same purpose, though their methods and appearance are far removed from their nautical namesakes of yesteryear. Notable pirate: Blackbeard.

CORSAIR

A corsair was a **pirate or privateer operating in the Mediterranean.** They were commonly Muslims from the Barbary Coast of North Africa, and their targets were ships of Christian countries. While religion was an instigating factor in their robberies, eventually it became just about the loot. Sometimes *corsair* is used synonymously with *privateer*. Notable corsair: Barbarossa.

RELATED TERM: *A term often used for pirates, a* **swashbuckler** *is a sword-wielding adventurer with gusto. Swash can mean "to dash" or "to swagger," and buckler is a word for "shield". Thus, swashbuckler suggests a guy dashing a sword against a shield.*

PRIVATEER

A privateer was a pirate with a **mandate from a government** to seize cargo from merchant ships of other nations. The term also referred to his ship, which was not part of a navy. The mandate was called a *letter of marque* (which means "frontier"). Rather than getting paid up front, privateers usually split the take with—and received safe harbor from—the government they worked for. A privateer was essentially a **legitimatized thief,** though the legitimacy depended on which side of the gangplank you were on. Because letters of marque were recognized by international law, a privateer was theoretically exempt from being charged with piracy. However, that didn't stop certain governments from bringing the charges anyway—one country's privateer was another's pirate, his tactics commensurate to an act of war. Some pirates and buccaneers dabbled in privateering at times. Many people considered privateers to be as unredeemable as pirates. Notable privateers: John Paul Jones, Alexander Selkirk (real-life inspiration for Robinson Crusoe), and Sir Francis Drake; sometimes Sir Henry Morgan is considered one, too.

BUCCANEER

A buccaneer was a **butcher turned pirate who operated in the Caribbean.** Many were French, but some were English or Dutch. Buccaneers killed wild pigs and domesticated cattle on Hispaniola, the island that is now Haiti and the Dominican Republic. They then smoked the meat and sold it to sailing crews, since ships had no way to refrigerate. The word *buccaneer* comes from *boucan*, the French word for the type of grill they used. Spain (which controlled Hispaniola) grew tired of the buccaneers' practice of stealing from their plantations, so they killed some and drove others off the island. These boar hunters then went after a different kind of prey—the Spanish. They aligned with others who had a grudge against the Spanish, based themselves on another island called Tortuga, and went to work getting payback on Spanish vessels in the West Indies. Notable buccaneer: Sir Henry Morgan.

What's the difference?

FOOD

APPLE JUICE and APPLE CIDER

CAFÉ AU LAIT, CAFÉ LATTE, and CAPPUCCINO

CHERRY TOMATO and GRAPE TOMATO

DINNER and SUPPER

FREE-RANGE, GRASS-FED, and PASTURED

FRUIT and VEGETABLE

JELLY, JAM, PRESERVES, and MARMALADE

SELTZER, CLUB SODA, and TONIC WATER

VANILLA and FRENCH VANILLA

WHITE EGG and BROWN EGG

What's the difference between...
APPLE JUICE and APPLE CIDER?

Apple juice and apple cider may not be as all-American as apple pie, but for the sake of clarity, what follows focuses on the terms as generally used in the United States. Their principal similarity is right there in the name—both are made from apples (100 percent, in fact). Their differences get a bit trickier; in fact, some insist that there is no difference between the two other than appearance. A traditional explanation: apple juice is commercial, apple cider is homemade. But that distinction, if it ever was true, is now a thing of the past.

APPLE JUICE	APPLE CIDER
Apple juice is a **filtered, clear liquid** made from mashed and pressed apples.	Apple cider is a frequently **unfiltered, caramel-colored, cloudy liquid** made from mashed and pressed apples. Suspended pulp is typically present.
It is almost always **pasteurized,** and labeled as such if not, as per FDA requirements. Apple juice does not require refrigeration before opening and therefore has a longer shelf life than cider.	Many **store-bought ciders now come pasteurized,** but jugs bought at road-side stands often aren't. Either way, cider should be refrigerated at all times.
Apple juice is sweet, endearing it to kids from sippy cup to juice box to straight-from-the-bottle (and maybe contributing to a cavity or two along the way, due to its **high sugar content**).	Some mills and manufacturers specify that their apple cider is made from an early-harvest blend of apples, which boosts its **tartness.**

Every fall on the East Coast, some apple juices undergo a transformation and become apple ciders. Actually, only their labels do—manufacturers know that "cider" has more of an autumn feel. But on the West Coast, the term "apple cider" is rarely seen, in any season.

RELATED TERM: *In many countries, "apple cider" connotes an alcoholic drink. In the United States, apple juice that has fermented to the point of becoming alcoholic is usually known as* **hard cider.**

Apples / Oranges

Next time someone tells you "It's like comparing apples to oranges," by which he means that two items you're looking at are radically different, call him on it. Say, "Oh, yeah? Why, because they're both fruits (see page 50)? And both edible fruits? And both fruits that grow on trees? And both roundish? And both able to fit in the palm of your hand? And both with juices named after them? And both on the warm side of the color spectrum?"

What's the difference between...
CAFÉ AU LAIT, CAFFE LATTE, and CAPPUCCINO?

Before the answer, another question: What's the difference between pre- and post-Starbucks coffee breaks? Before Starbucks, you just ordered "coffee."

The posher coffee drinks require more knowledge of fraction—and thermal physics (but we'll leave the vagaries of precise temperatures to the baristas.) The following seem to be standard breakdowns of each hot beverage, though you'll find variations from café to café.

CAFÉ AU LAIT

Café au lait is one-third **dark roast coffee** (drip or filter method) and two-thirds **scalded milk.** In some cases, espresso is used instead of coffee. A café au lait is commonly served in a twelve-ounce (355 ml) white bowl, which you hold with both hands to sip.

CAFFE LATTE

Caffe latte is one-third **espresso** and two-thirds **steamed (heated) milk.** To some, it's just the Italian version of the French café au lait, but others claim that caffe latte is different because it's made with steamed—not scalded—milk. It's also similar to the Spanish café con leche. A proper caffe latte has no foam, though some American coffee shops top it with frothed (heated and aerated) milk, making it veer close to cappuccino territory. A café latte is usually served in a tall clear glass.

CAPPUCCINO

A classic cappuccino consists of **espresso** and **foamed (sometimes frothed) milk.** Some places serve a cappuccino of one-third espresso, one-third steamed milk, and one-third foamed milk. The milk separates, with the steamed milk sinking to the bottom and the foam floating to the top. It's less mild than a caffe latte. Flavorings such as powdered cinnamon or cocoa powder are possible additions, but not essential components of a cappuccino. Known for their creaminess, cappuccinos are popular breakfast and dessert drinks (though never taken for dessert in Italy), and are usually served in a seven-ounce (207 ml) ceramic cup.

RELATED TERM: Espresso, *a strong, thick brew served as a drink in and of itself, is also the base of caffe latte, cappuccino, and sometimes café au lait.*

What's the difference between...
a CHERRY TOMATO and a GRAPE TOMATO?

Small, roundish, scrumptious, and red. No, not Skittles...tomatoes! At the turn of the millennium, the title of top tiny tomato, long held by the cherry tomato, was snatched away by one of its protégés, the grape tomato.

CHERRY TOMATO

A cherry tomato is an **orb-shaped fruit** (see page 50) about one inch in diameter and available in red, orange, yellow, and green varieties. These tomatoes are sweeter than beefsteak and globe tomatoes. They've been around since before cultivation. To make them easier to eat, they usually need to be **cut in half.** Cherry tomatoes are actually a family of tomatoes, and also include pear tomatoes (sometimes known as teardrop tomatoes) and a relatively new addition, grape tomatoes.

GRAPE TOMATO

A grape tomato is a **grape-shaped fruit** ½ to ¾ inch (1.3 to 1.9 cm) long; it's almost always red. Grape tomatoes are a tad **sweeter** than their cherry relatives, and typically smaller. No knife need touch these little gems to make them eater friendly—they pop right in the mouth whole, eliminating the squirt factor. Plus, in salads, they're **easier to spear** with a fork than cherry tomatoes. They were first grown successfully in the United States in 1996 and debuted as a specialty item. Consumers rapidly became enamored of them, and they are poised to overtake cherry tomatoes in sales. Grape tomatoes now appear in most stores where produce is sold, not just in upscale markets.

Tomato/"Tomahto"
You say "tomato." Someone pompous says "tomahto."

What's the difference between…
DINNER and SUPPER?

Peek in on different eras, cultures, and social classes and you'll see that these terms have had several different meanings over the years. So as not to spoil your dinner (or supper) with a heavy history lesson, let's just stick to the most current, popular interpretations of the terms.

DINNER

Dinner is the **main meal of the day,** though when that main meal is consumed depends on the region. In some areas, people eat dinner at midday. This is a more common usage in the rural South and patches of the Midwest. Meanwhile, most urbanites associate dinner with night and know the midday meal as lunch. (Further adding to this perplexing smorgasbord of variations, *dinner* was once a word for—believe it or not—"breakfast.")

In everyday life, the word *dinner* can denote a casual meal, but it is also the word more commonly used to refer to **formal meals,** and indeed a dinner often comprises several courses. One hears of "dinner parties" but rarely if ever "supper parties." Grand-scale political fundraising events are dinners, not suppers. And, of course, Thanksgiving is a dinner, not a supper.

SUPPER

Supper is the **last meal of the day,** eaten in the early evening (if dinner is at midday) or just before bedtime (if dinner is later than midday). Either way, supper is **lighter than dinner.** So according to the latter meaning, if you were ever sent to bed without dinner, or you've done that to your kids, you (and they) could've requested supper first—and they'd be entitled to it.

In simpler times, a supper club was an intimate stopover between catching a play and calling it a night. Today, supper generally has a **cozier connotation** than dinner. Despite these distinctions, in many parts of America, *supper* and *dinner* are synonymous and refer to the main evening meal.

What's the difference between...
FREE-RANGE, GRASS-FED, and PASTURED?

Before you eat that chicken, know what it ate. And under what conditions it ate it. To do that, you need to understand what these terms reveal—and what they don't.

FREE-RANGE

Free-range is a nonstandardized and **misleading term** regarding the way poultry is raised, conjuring idyllic images of the birds blissfully pecking around in unending green fields. In truth, free-range is defined as a system in which chickens have **access to the outdoors**—whether or not they actually go outdoors, and whether or not that outdoors is luscious grass, a patch of dirt, or even concrete. Though consumers seem to trust that this term on chicken packaging means quality, it is sometimes abused. Many free-range chickens are mostly coop-dwellers that don't get any living greens in their diet.

GRASS-FED

Grass-fed describes poultry that subsist largely on grasses rather than grain. These chickens are often kept in **small coops surrounded by pasture.** Much packaged meat comes from large confinement facilities where the animals are pumped with chemicals and fattened only with grains, a tactic that has been linked to degenerative disease in humans. Grass-fed birds are healthier and generally yield more tender meat (the same is true of beef, but let's save that discussion for another time). The grass gives the birds (and later people) valuable nutrients, notably omega-3 fatty acids. Though some farms claim that they feed their chickens grass exclusively, experts say chickens cannot live on grass alone and also need some grain.

PASTURED

Pastured is a subset of *grass-fed*. It describes poultry grazing on living grasses and insects via a system of **portable, bottomless pens.** And as with grass-fed birds, they do need some grain, too. Though this system does involve confinement, that doesn't mean crowding—many pastured chickens are members of small flocks on small farms. The pens are used primarily to protect the birds from predators. They're moved regularly (typically once or twice a day) to ensure a fresh supply of grass and to prevent the birds from stepping in their own droppings. Because the birds are also getting exercise this way, they develop more muscle, which can enhance their flavor. Be aware that "grass-fed" doesn't automatically mean "pastured," and vice versa.

RELATED TERMS: *As customers get more discriminating and food marketers become savvier, new and often unclear terms flood the shelves:* **"cage-free," "free-farmed,"** *and so on. Before taking a package label's word, do a little research about nomenclature and specific farms to find out what the terms mean. For example, some chickens labeled* **"organic"** *may still be treated inhumanely although they're given organic feed.*

What's the difference between...
a FRUIT and a VEGETABLE?

If it's found in cereal or ice cream, it's a fruit, and if your younger self was forced to stay at the table until you'd eaten it, it's a vegetable, right? Let's dig a little deeper (or pick a little higher, depending).

FRUIT	VEGETABLE
To a botanist, a fruit is the **ripened ovary of a flowering plant**—the fleshy substance that covers the seed or seeds. While "fleshy substance" is catchy and all, we're lucky that "fruit" sounded a smidge more appetizing to whoever named these things.	Vegetables are other edible parts of a plant, including the **roots, stem, leaves, seeds, and bulbs.**
Fruits are known for being **sweet,** but not *all* fruits are sweet. Tomatoes, avocados, cucumbers, squashes, zucchini, and peapods aren't as sweet as, say, a peach. (And, yes, despite what you thought until a sentence ago, they're all fruits. That may have shocked you more than a broccoli and cauliflower smoothie would.)	To grocery stores and the average shopper, the unscientific difference between fruits and vegetables is how and when we eat them. Vegetables aren't sweet, so they're **"serious" food**—for meals, not desserts. Perhaps some of those protests in which you defiantly stared at your untouched dinner (see page 47) until midnight were misguided. If only you knew then that it's not where they're found on a plate that separates fruits from vegetables. It's where they're found on a plant.

Fruits that are sweet attract animals, which carry them off and therefore help spread their seeds. Their sweetness is a sneaky survival strategy.

LIFE/Life/Life (in the Commercial Sense)

The meaning of Life comes down to whether you want to read, play, or eat. LIFE was a photojournalism magazine that was first published in 1936 as a weekly. In 1978, it became a monthly, and ceased publication in 2000. In 2004, it was reborn as a free weekly newspaper supplement. The Game of Life (commonly shortened to Life) is a board game originally produced by Milton Bradley (now part of Hasbro) that debuted in 1960. Life Cereal from Quaker Oats hit shelves in 1961; Cinnamon Life followed in 1978, Honey Graham Life in 2004. Seemingly ideal yet unexplored co-branding opportunities exist here. Let's see what develops.

What's the difference between...
JELLY, JAM, PRESERVES, and MARMALADE?

Peanut butter actually has a choice of partners. They're all made from fruit (see page 50) in some form, from whole to pulverized, and some are also supplemented with sugar.

JELLY

Jelly is a spread made from **fruit juice cooked with sugar and often pectin,** which is a chemical that helps a liquid jell into a semisolid. Some fruits, including raspberries and apples, contain enough natural pectin to do this, while others, such as strawberries and cherries, need an assist from other fruits or artificial pectin. After processing, jelly is clear and free of pulp. When removed from the jar, it's firm enough to hold its shape. It can be either sweet or savory, though kids don't want to hear about the latter.

JAM

Jam is a spread made from fruit itself, a blend of **crushed pieces and puree.** The ingredients are "jammed" together and boiled. It, too, holds its shape, but not as much as jelly.

PRESERVES

Preserves are a concoction of **whole fruit or fruit chunks and syrup,** often slightly jellied. They are thicker than jellies and jams.

MARMALADE

Marmalade is a **jelly containing shreds of citrus fruit rind,** or sometimes pieces of other fruits. The rind or bits of evenly sized fruit are suspended in a clear jelly.

RELATED TERM: Conserves *are jams thick with citrus fruit and nuts. Some contain raisins or coconut.*

What's the difference between...
SELTZER, CLUB SODA, and TONIC WATER?

Keeping track of the subtle differences between these clear bubblies can make anyone dizzy. If you still can't tell Coke and Pepsi apart, just move right along to the next entry.

SELTZER

Seltzer (or seltzer water) is a **flavorless effervescent beverage** named after Nieder Selters, a German town. Originally, seltzer was naturally effervescent, but now humans produce it by injecting water with carbon dioxide. In the mid-1800s, flavors were added to seltzer, a process that evolved into the juggernaut known as the soft drink. Confuse seltzer with any other drink in this entry and no harm is done; just don't confuse it with Alka-Seltzer.

CLUB SODA

Club soda (sometimes called soda water) is a flavorless soft drink that also gets its effervescence from an infusion of carbon dioxide. The distinction between seltzer and club soda is that club soda also **contains a bit of sodium bicarbonate,** lending it a neutralizing quality for upset stomachs. Despite this difference, club soda is sometimes used synonymously with seltzer.

TONIC WATER

Tonic water (or Indian tonic water, so called for the country where British colonists began to enjoy it) is yet another fizzy soft drink, this one **containing quinine.** This bark extract was added to carbonated water to help prevent malaria, and gave it a bitter taste. Commercial tonic water today still contains quinine, but not enough to be medicinal.

RELATED TERMS: Mineral water *is effervescent water mixed with sodium, calcium, iron, gases, or other substances (whether naturally or artificially) and purported to have therapeutic effects.*

Sparkling water *is a name for several types of carbonated water on the market with deceptively similar descriptions; some are naturally effervescent mineral waters, some are artificially effervescent mineral waters, and some artificially carbonated—but not mineral—waters.*

Ginger ale *is a ginger-flavored soft drink that, like club soda, sometimes serves as a home remedy for stomachs in topsy-turvy mode.*

It would be too easy to reveal that French vanilla is neither French nor vanilla. But we're left with no choice (unlike when we're standing in front of the ice cream freezer in the supermarket, drooling at the eighty-three equally tempting varieties).

Vanilla is a **flavoring derived from vanilla beans,** which are fruits from a plant in the orchid family. These plants are native to Mexico, but today are grown throughout the tropics, notably in Madagascar. You probably know vanilla as the perennial best-selling flavor of ice cream, despite the fact that "vanilla" often describes something (or someone) bland.

French vanilla is **not a type of vanilla.** It's more like fantasy vanilla: when shown a copy-paper-white scoop of ice cream and a pastel yellow scoop that is flecked with black, which do you gravitate toward? The one that seems more authentic, or at least more romantic in some ethereal way—the bean-flecked yellow. "French vanilla" refers to a **precooked custard loaded with egg yolks** that is used as the base for the ice cream that takes its name. Many feel that French vanilla is more aromatic than vanilla, and while it may be, it's not likely the vanilla that makes it so.

What's the difference between...
a WHITE EGG and a BROWN EGG?

After "Which came first?" this is the most hotly debated chicken and egg question. (Come to think of it, this may be the *only* other hotly debated chicken and egg question.) The answer is much less tricky: eggshell color is determined by the breed of the hen.

WHITE EGG	BROWN EGG
White eggs come from hens with **white feathers** (and, oddly, white earlobes). Members of this crowd are White Leghorn chickens.	Brown (or brown-speckled) eggs come from hens with **reddish brown feathers** (and, again, earlobes to match). This bunch includes Rhode Island Red, New Hampshire, and Plymouth Rock chickens.
Though the taste doesn't vary according to color, consumer preferences do. Far more white eggs are sold in the United States than brown eggs.	Brown eggs are particularly popular in New England. But they cost more simply because brown hens tend to be bigger, and therefore eat more, which costs the farmers more, and that cost is passed on to the consumer.

Since brown eggs are usually more expensive, some people believe they're more healthful, or more "natural." Nutritionally, however, and in all other ways save color, white and brown eggs are the same.

What's the difference?

SOCIETY

COLLEGE and UNIVERSITY

DEMOCRACY and REPUBLIC

MEMORIAL DAY and VETERANS DAY

MORALITY and ETHICS

STATE and COMMONWEALTH

What's the difference between…
a COLLEGE and a UNIVERSITY?

The meanings of these terms vary from country to country. What is typically known as a college in Europe would be the equivalent of a two-year community college or vocational school in the United States.

In the United States, the terms are usually used interchangeably, and much about them can indeed be similar. For example, both can be either public or private. But there are some nuances.

COLLEGE

A college is an institution that a student attends for four years to earn a **bachelor's degree** (or sometimes an associate's degree, which takes less time). They are frequently **smaller** than universities and don't typically have a research component, allowing teachers to give students more time and individualized attention. Historically, a college was a collection of people pursuing a common course of study and living in a clustered environment. Today, schools such as Dartmouth and Boston retain "college" in their name even though they have the characteristics of a university. Besides the headache of reprinting all the course catalogs and T-shirts, they may choose to remain a college in homage to the British institutions on which they're based. In some cases, such as at Harvard, "college" refers solely to the undergraduate division of a school, while "university" includes that college and all the other divisions.

RELATED TERMS: *Sometimes colleges and universities are not called colleges and universities.* **"Institute"** *(Massachusetts Institute of Technology),* **"academy"** *(United States Military Academy at West Point), or even just* **"school"** *(Juilliard School) can step in and do the job.*

UNIVERSITY

A university is also a four-year institution offering undergraduate degrees, but they offer advanced degrees such as **master's and doctoral degrees as well.** Universities often consist of multiple colleges, such as a business college, nursing college, or teaching college, and therefore grant a **wider range of degrees.** The faculty often divide their time between teaching and research.

D-Plus / D / D-Minus

In school, did you ever really have the chutzpah to announce you got a D-plus (emphasis on plus), as if that somehow made your feat more impressive? A pinch of advice: when you're on the verge of failing, don't embarrass yourself further by pretending those few measly points closer to a below-average grade actually matter. That kind of delusion gives slackers a bad name.

What's the difference between...
a DEMOCRACY and a REPUBLIC?

Of all the differences in this book, this is the one you're probably most embarrassed to admit you can't explain despite the fact that it was covered practically every year in school. Here's a teaser: the United States is not a democracy, just as the Founding Fathers intended. The difference comes down to who's got the authority. (Doesn't it always?)

In 1787, James Madison wrote in the Federalist Paper 14, "The true distinction between these forms…is that in a democracy, the people meet and exercise the government in person; in a republic they assemble and administer it by their representatives and agents. A democracy, consequently, must be confined to a **small spot.** A republic may be extended over a **large region.**"

In a democracy, **majority rules.** In a republic, the **rights of the individual rule.** In a democracy, the masses can outweigh the individual, whereas in a republic, no group can override the rights of any single citizen. Some even liken democracy to mob rule—whether the mob's opinion is "right" or "wrong." But a republic is rule by law as decided by the entire population.

A democratic government can become a tyranny—tyranny of the majority. A republican government doesn't have power *over* its citizens—it gets its power *from* its citizens. It says so in the Declaration of Independence, right after mentioning the pursuit of happiness. Democratic governments **grant rights, and can take them away.** Republican governments **see rights as unalienable, and protect them.**

Both democracies and republics can have elected leaders, but in democracies, those leaders can set law on their own—like a monarchy. While a democracy can have royalty, a republic has no hereditary rulers such as kings and queens.

That doesn't preclude a so-called republic being ruled by a dictator, who is sometimes a person who seizes control, but sometimes a person chosen by the people who then rules by force.

A true democracy would not be practical for the United States—or any body larger than a town hall meeting, really. Would you want to keep abreast of every matter of government and be expected to vote on something every day? We elect legislators to do that with our interests in mind, and all citizens—including government officials—are subject to the same laws. Therefore, the United States is not a direct democracy but a republic governed by a representative democracy.

If the United States' classification still doesn't sound familiar, here's something that will: recite the Pledge of Allegiance. Ah—"…and to the *republic* for which it stands…" Or sing the "Battle Hymn of the Democracy." Wait, that's "Battle Hymn of the *Republic*." Or just read the Declaration and the Constitution. Neither describes America as a "democracy"—neither even uses the word. Looks like the clues have been there all along.

What's the difference between...
MEMORIAL DAY and VETERANS DAY?

This may shatter all you thought you knew about three-day weekends: the United States has no national holidays. What it does have are federal holidays—days on which government employees don't have to work. As for who else gets to follow suit, it's up to each state (see page 68) and each company. Both of these are federal holidays, though unless you're employed by the government, you probably get only Memorial Day off. However, you're about to be reminded that these observances are about honoring the brave service of others—whether or not you're on the clock.

MEMORIAL DAY

Memorial Day is a holiday observed on the **last Monday of May.** First proclaimed Decoration Day in 1868 in reference to the practice of decorating soldiers' graves with flowers, its name was changed to Memorial Day in 1882. It was founded to pay tribute to those who were killed in the American Civil War, but after World War I the focus changed to **all soldiers who had died in or as a result of any war.** Yet it was only after World War II that Memorial Day began to gain national prominence; it went into effect as a federal holiday in 1971. Today, some people also take it as an opportunity to acknowledge all loved ones who have died, including civilians.

VETERANS DAY

Veterans Day is a holiday observed every **November 11,** regardless of what day of the week that is. Established in 1919 to mark the first anniversary of the end of hostilities of World War I (then called the Great War), it was originally dubbed Armistice Day. It became a federal holiday in 1938 and soon evolved into a day for honoring **everyone–living or dead–who has served in the armed forces,** during times of war or peace. In doing so, it underwent a name change to Veterans (no apostrophe) Day in 1954, and not just because nobody remembered what "armistice" means. Though Veterans Day does honor all American soldiers, some people feel that the emphasis of the day should be to thank those who are still living, partly to further distinguish it from Memorial Day.

What's the difference between...
MORALITY and ETHICS?

There may be as much debate over morality and ethics as there is between right and wrong. Some chalk up the difference to word root alone—*morals* from the Latin *moralis* and *ethics* from the Greek *ethos*. In casual conversation—though when is a discussion of this topic casual?—the terms are often used interchangeably. However, it would be right to say that's wrong.

Morals are **beliefs regarding appropriate behavior.** This can vary widely from person to person and society to society. Ethics is the **formal study of morality.** The field is sometimes called "moral philosophy." Among the big questions posed in ethics are "What is good?" and "What is evil?" and "What is right?" and "What is wrong?" This "appropriate" behavior is frequently described as "good" or "right." Ethics is an intellectual approach to those concepts.

We form moral judgments about other people regarding their character and their conduct, particularly at moments when they must make a choice. If a person kicked a puppy because he had nothing else to do, most of us would consider that immoral. But if a person kicked a puppy because that puppy lunged in his direction with its teeth bared, it changes our perspective. That person had to make a quick choice—do nothing and be bitten or defend himself. Sure, he had other options—jump to the side, throw up his arms, run, scream—but he reacted in the way that he thought would most likely spare him from stitches.

An outsider who observed and then evaluated this scenario would be applying ethics. We often make our judgments based on standards that society has established. If this incident took place in a society in which kicking puppies is not acceptable under any circumstances, the outsider might conclude that the

Right/Wrong

The answer is straightforward, actually. First, people who are right are always able to admit it, whereas people who are wrong are not. Next, if you're married, your opinion is always right as opposed to your spouse's, which, according to the oldest marriage custom, is always wrong. Otherwise, it depends on whether you have a cape (stereotypical hero) or a maniacal laugh (stereotypical villain). In Superman's mind, his actions are right and Lex Luthor's are wrong. In Lex Luthor's mind, he's doing the right thing while Superman, by thwarting him, is the one who is wrong. Few people are the villains of their own stories.

kicker was wrong. Or if it happened in a society that allows extreme actions taken in self-defense, be it against a puppy, another person, or a great white shark, the outsider might conclude that the kicker was morally entitled to do what he did.

Our morals are also based on what we value personally. If we value human life over nonhuman life, then the kicker is vindicated in our minds. If we consider all forms of life equal, then it becomes a question of why the puppy attacked. Was he provoked or just belligerent by nature? If provoked, then maybe the guy deserved a flesh wound. If belligerent, then even some animal rights activists may agree that the kicker is again absolved.

Some people make a different distinction between morals and ethics. They might claim that morals are a person's personal beliefs about upstanding behavior and ethics are society's. Morals are **based on influences** that include culture, religion, and family. Ethics are **universal**—think golden rules. As such, someone may feel that drinking alcohol is immoral while recognizing that society does not consider it unethical (if done responsibly, of course).

What's the difference between...
a STATE and a COMMONWEALTH?

To prepare for this answer, you need a clarification. (Warning: you'll vehemently deny it at first.) America is made up of forty-six states. No, this is not a typo or a fact from a 1908 textbook. It's a matter of semantics in the here and now.

Officially, **Virginia, Massachusetts, Pennsylvania, and Kentucky** are commonwealths, not states. However, this sense of the word *commonwealth* is synonymous with the sense of the word *state* as used in *United States*. In all respects other than name, a commonwealth and a state are **legally the same.**

Here's some historical background: after the execution of King Charles I in 1649, Oliver Cromwell became the leader (not king) of England (see page 132). His new government, which lasted until 1660, was called the *Commonwealth,* which means "for the common good of the people." The colonists in Virginia, Massachusetts, Pennsylvania, and Kentucky, who weren't very keen on monarchy, seemingly liked the rebellious spirit of the term. After the American Revolution, those four opted to use that designation for their own parcels of land, possibly to recall Cromwell's government or to further distance themselves from Great Britain, which was then called a "state."

The four commonwealths stuck with that word even when their neighbors were deciding it'd look less ostentatious to have "state" on their official letterhead. In 1787, Pennsylvania became the second state (uh, first commonwealth) of the Union. Massachusetts was sixth and Virginia tenth, both in 1788. Kentucky was part of Virginia until 1792, when it split off and became the fifteenth commonwealth-presumed-to-be-state. And none of the four has changed its mind.

In terms of U.S. politics, another sense of the word *commonwealth* does differ from *state*. Puerto Rico and the Northern Mariana Islands are also called commonwealths of the United States. These self-governing, unincorporated territories have voluntarily aligned with the United States, but they don't possess statehood, meaning that their citizens don't vote in presidential elections or pay federal taxes. Some factions within these commonwealths have lobbied to become states.

Hell/Hell on Earth

When you're condemned to burn for your sins for all eternity, it's comforting to know you have a choice about where to do it. Oh—you didn't know? Yes, there's the traditional hell, the one as far down as you can do without starting to go back up again. And then there's hell *on* Earth, whose location is a carefully guarded secret but is rumored to be in the most unforgiving section of the Amazon rainforest, at the exact center of the punishing Sahara Desert, or somewhere on the Upper East Side of Manhattan. Regardless, it's a lot easier to get to than the flagship location, though the taxes (and sometimes, believe it or not, the humidity) are worse. Bear in mind that once you decide, they won't transfer you—unless you love where you are.

HUMAN BODY, INSIDE AND OUT

ARTERY and VEIN

CANKER SORE and COLD SORE

EMBRYO and FETUS

PERFUME, EAU DE PERFUME,
EAU DE TOILETTE, and EAU DE COLOGNE

PLAQUE and TARTAR

SPRAIN and STRAIN

SUNSCREEN and SUNBLOCK

What's the difference between...
an ARTERY and a VEIN?

Arteries get clogged. Veins get varicose. Anything else? Your heart says yes.

ARTERY

An artery is a blood vessel through which blood flows **away from the heart** to cells, tissues, and organs.

The walls of an artery are **thick and muscular,** and it's a good thing, too. They need to be able to handle how vigorously the heart pumps out blood—plus some of that blood needs to be pumped against gravity, up to our heads.

VEIN

A vein is a blood vessel through which blood flows **to the heart** from the rest of the body.

Vein walls are **thin and membranous.** Less muscular than artery walls, they close in when empty.

RELATED TERM: *A* **capillary** *is the slimmest of blood vessels. It's no thicker than a red blood cell. Nourishing substances including oxygen and glucose can pass through capillaries to surrounding tissues. Capillaries connect to the larger blood vessels in the circulatory system.*

Veins don't have the pronounced pulsating sensation that arteries do. When you check your pulse, it's an artery telegraphing you that vital stat.

Arterial blood is **oxygenated,** having passed through the lungs. The exception: the blood in the pulmonary artery, which carries deoxygenated blood from the heart to the lungs.

Venous blood is heading back to headquarters—the heart—to replenish its oxygen supply. The pulmonary vein is the only one that transports oxygenated blood, from the lungs to the heart. Because the **blood in veins contains less oxygen** than the blood in arteries, it's darker. Unlike arteries, some veins have **one-way valves** to prevent blood backflow. That's especially important in your extremities, from which blood must travel the farthest. Blood courses through veins at **lower pressure and slower pace** than it does through arteries. Veins tend to be **wider** and hold more blood than arteries—which is why medical folks with needles draw blood from them and not from arteries.

What's the difference between...
a CANKER SORE and a COLD SORE?

Canker sores are easier to hide from others than cold sores. Unfortunately, cold sores are more embarrassing and therefore the ones you *want* to hide.

CANKER SORE	COLD SORE
A canker sore (more ominously known as an aphthous ulcer) is a painful irritation on the mucous membrane **inside the mouth.** It looks like a white oval ringed by red.	A cold sore (otherwise known as a fever blister or—yikes—herpes simplex) is a painful irritation **outside the mouth,** typically on the lips, under the nose, or somewhere else in the key kissing region. It's composed of fluid-filled blisters that can resemble pimples or insect bites.
The **cause of canker sores is uncertain,** but stress, nutritional deficiency, and food allergies are among the possible causes. Canker sores can also form when you bite your lip or tongue.	Cold sores are **caused by the herpes simplex virus,** usually type 1 but sometimes type 2. Type 1 usually occurs on the face and type 2 in the genital area, though both can infect either site.
They're common, they're **not known to be contagious,** and they typically go away on their own in about a week.	Cold sores are **contagious**—both to other mouths and to genitals. Transmission can happen in ways other than oral sex. For example, contact can occur via a hand that touches the infected mouth and then the unsuspecting private area. Like canker sores, cold sores are common and can heal within a week—but even that's not nearly fast enough for many people who have them.

What's the difference between...
an EMBRYO and a FETUS?

For centuries, attempts to answer this question have played out in two arenas: science and morality (see page 66). To call this an emotional subject is an understatement, and that is a good sign. It shows that people on every side of the issue are urgently concerned about the sanctity of life.

EMBRYO	FETUS
A human embryo is a human in the womb at the **earliest stage of its development**—from conception to the eighth (some say sixth) week.	A human fetus is a developing human from the **eighth week to birth.** (In some definitions, *fetus* refers exclusively to an unborn human.) Although a full-term pregnancy lasts forty weeks, "fetus" can also be applied to humans who are born earlier. (But at that point, most parents would probably prefer "baby"!)
Organs begin to form in this embryonic stage.	The bulk of **organ maturation occurs** after an organism passes the threshold between embryo and fetus.
In appearance, embryos **don't resemble humans,** but the genetic material in an embryo is the same as in a centenarian.	Fetuses start off as small as baked beans, but even then they **look like scrunched-up human babies.**

RELATED TERM: Stem cells *are unspecialized cells that can go on to produce any type of specialized cell in the body. Some experts posit that embryonic stem cells are living organisms while others say they're not, a distinction at the core of an impassioned controversy.*

What's the difference between…
PERFUME, EAU DE PARFUM, EAU DE TOILETTE, and EAU DE COLOGNE?

Perfumes are mixtures that include redolent essential oils from plants and synthetic materials, some of which intensify the smell and increase its longevity. The liquid base of perfumes is alcohol. The ratio of scents to alcohol determines which type of fragrance the blend will be. The higher the amount of oils (or "juice"), the more potent the scent—and the more expensive the perfume will be. Also, more juice means that you can apply less and that the fragrance will linger longer.

PERFUME

Perfume has the highest concentration of aromatic essence, typically between **15 and 30 percent** of the formulation. It also has the least amount of alcohol. Perfume is the purest and priciest of the scents. It's generally **dabbed rather than sprayed** onto the skin. Depending on skin type, the fragrance can last up to six hours.

EAU DE PARFUM

Eau de parfum is the most prevalent type of perfume. It contains **8 to 15 percent** aromatic essence. For best effect, it should be **judiciously applied** on the skin's warmest patches, including the wrists and collarbone and, if you've got a certain type of night planned, between the breasts and on the inner thighs. It lasts three to five hours.

For every odor, there is a fragrance strong enough to cover it up, though not necessarily a budget big enough to pay for it.

EAU DE TOILETTE

Eau de toilette has **4 to 8 percent** aromatic essence. This type of scent was designed to be **splashed** over the body in the morning to awaken and refresh. It's the perfume most suited to everyday use, and it lasts two to four hours.

EAU DE COLOGNE

Eau de cologne (often just called cologne) contains **3 to 5 percent** aromatic essence. It's the perfume type most commonly associated with male use, and is generally **sprayed or dabbed** on. Napoleon was a huge fan of cologne, and he popularized its use in France. It lasts only two hours. No wonder Napoleon went through eight quarts a month.

What's the difference between...

PLAQUE and TARTAR?

A plaque is a flat wall hanging, often a piece of engraved metal mounted on board, used to commemorate or honor a person, group, or institution. Tartar is a type of sauce made from mayonnaise and chopped pickles. The two are not usually confused—oh, right, unless you're talking dentally.

PLAQUE

Plaque is a **soft deposit of bacteria** that adheres to and gets stuck between teeth daily. It can begin to settle on your choppers as quickly as four hours after brushing. By some accounts it's white and by others colorless, but either way, it's hard to see. The acids in plaque can lead to tooth decay, gum disease, or even tooth loss.

Regular brushing and flossing is designed to **remove plaque**—which gives both you and your dentist reason to smile.

TARTAR

Tartar, also known as calculus, is **hardened plaque.** When the bacteria interact with saliva and food particles, particularly sugars and starches, tartar forms at the gum line through a process called calcification. The crusty, yellowish brown substance creates a surface hospitable for further bacterial growth. About the most positive thing tartar can do is stain teeth. The average person is powerless to remove it.

Regular brushing and especially flossing will **reduce the formation** of tartar in your mouth, but only the wizardry of a dental professional can free your teeth from tartar buildup.

What's the difference between...
a SPRAIN and a STRAIN?

This could've instead been the difference between ligaments and tendons, but come on—it's more perversely interesting to talk about body injuries than body parts. (Okay: ligaments connect bones to other bones to form a joint, while tendons connect bones to muscles. Happy?)

SPRAIN

A sprain is an injury to one or more **ligaments.** Twisted ankles and pulled muscles are sprains; knees and other bendable parts also suffer their unfair share. Ligaments are there to prevent abnormal movements, but they're obviously not invincible. When one is stretched too far, it can tear partially or completely.

STRAIN

A strain is an injury to a **tendon or muscle.** Among the more common strain sites are backs, necks, and thighs. Muscles are designed to stretch (and stretching muscles before exercise is one of the recommended ways to prevent strains as well as sprains), but they can go only so far. If their capacity is exceeded, they can tear.

Sprains and strains are considered minor injuries because they can heal quickly and often without medical intervention. You can strain yourself without spraining yourself, but when you sprain yourself, you're usually straining yourself, too.

What's the difference between...
SUNSCREEN and SUNBLOCK?

The sun is constantly sending several types of rays our way. All may put us in a good mood, but these invisible ultraviolet (UV) rays are damaging, too. UV-A rays are sometimes known as the "aging" rays because they wrinkle the skin. UV-B rays are sometimes called the "burn" rays. Beware: both rays can lead to both effects. And while both sunscreen and sunblock shield us from them, neither provides 100-percent protection. After all, they're not called sunburnscreen or skincancerblock.

SUNSCREEN	SUNBLOCK
Sunscreen **works chemically to filter** UV rays. Early sunscreens absorbed only UV-B, but modern science has given them oomph against UV-A, too. Sunscreen comes in creams, lotions, and gels, most of which are transparent (though slick looking) when rubbed in. For people with sensitive skin, sunscreen is often recommended more than sunblock.	Sunblock **works physically to deflect** UV rays. Ingredients include titanium dioxide and zinc oxide. Sunblock used to be conspicuous— think lifeguard noses. That thick stuff was also hard to wash off. Newer sunblocks can blend into skin better and are generally less goopy than they used to be.

RELATED TERMS: SPF 15 *sunscreen (the minimum dermatologists recommend) absorbs 93 percent of UV radiation. Slathered with SPF 15, you can remain in the sun without burning fifteen times longer than without it.* **SPF 30** *soaks up 97 percent— not 186 percent—so it's a mistake to assume that the sun protection factor numbers represent a proportional increase in protection.*

Water-resistant *sun protection products maintain their SPF level after you're in the water for forty minutes, while* **waterproof** *products do the same for up to eighty minutes of water exposure.*

Your Ass / Your Elbow

Hopefully no one has ever told you that "you don't know the difference between your ass and your elbow." If someone has, and you don't, here you go: your ass (or "buttocks," as the more folksy among us might say) is composed of muscle, while your elbow is a joint. The former you use to sit at the table, the latter you rudely rest on the table. It's possible but not recommended to reverse these positions.

A variation on this observation is "you don't know the difference between your ass and a hole in the ground." A hole in the ground is a spot where earth has been removed, leaving an empty space that someone might fall into if he's not careful. Since "ass" and "elbow" are both body parts, it's conceivable a person might jumble them. But a hole in the ground is not anatomical, so let's hope no one would ever really confuse it for a rear end.

What's the difference?

CRIME

BURGLARY and ROBBERY

HOMICIDE, MURDER, and MANSLAUGHTER

JUSTICE and REVENGE

PLEADING GUILTY and PLEADING NO CONTEST

What's the difference between...
BURGLARY and ROBBERY?

These crimes can almost be differentiated in terms of passive-aggressive thievery and just plain aggressive thievery, though victims of burglary might beg to differ.

BURGLARY

Burglary is the theft of property **without the owner being aware** of the crime while it is happening.

Burglary is linked to breaking and entering—so in that sense, burglary is specifically **related to a home or other building.** The degree of burglary usually depends on whether there is someone on the premises while the crime is in progress. Burglars have a reputation for staking out houses and waiting for the inhabitants to leave before going to work. Some legal systems define burglary as a night crime and may even carry lesser penalties for the same act if it occurs during daytime. However, the average person wouldn't be less ticked off just because his stuff was stolen while the sun was shining.

ROBBERY

Robbery is the theft of property by force or fear—meaning that the **robber confronts the owner-victim.**

Robberies are **not tied to any type of location,** such as a home, a store, or a bank. And it doesn't matter whether the robber really will resort to violence—or whether he even has a weapon. In either case, the threat of harm is enough to classify the crime as a robbery, specifically aggravated robbery. A robbery is colloquially known as a "stickup" or a "holdup."

Stop Sign / Stop Ahead Sign

In the United States, stop signs are red octagons displaying the word STOP printed in white. They are used exclusively to direct cars on roads (see page 139); you don't need to install them in public buildings or private homes. A less common sign is a yellow, diamond-shaped sign that depicts a small red octagon and an arrow pointing to the sky. This does not mean a falling stop sign is about to hit you. Rather it indicates that a regular stop sign is ahead but may not yet be visible. Thus, this sign is referred to as a stop ahead sign.

When you see this sign, it is best not to panic. Instead, remember what this sign is whispering: "Fear not. I am giving you time to come to a gradual stop so you will not screech uncontrollably into the intersection that lies ahead." We should all be thankful that stop ahead signs are out there. Daily, silently, and without need of praise, they stand as a key cog in the wheel that keeps vehicular chaos at bay.

RELATED TERM: Breaking and entering *is illegally going into someone else's property, even if the intruder doesn't literally break anything to do it. Opening an unlocked door doesn't change the fact that it's a crime. If done without criminal intent, it can be ruled as trespassing, which is usually a misdemeanor. If done with criminal intent, it becomes a burglary, which is usually a felony.*

HOMICIDE, MURDER, and MANSLAUGHTER?

If you've killed time, your career, or your chances with your single and sexy new neighbor, you'll have to deal with the consequences yourself. For the consequences of other kinds of killing, society takes over.

HOMICIDE

Homicide is the **killing** of one human being by another. It's the blanket term for all such acts. It's also a **neutral term**—it does not involve passing judgment on the reason for the killing—which is probably why we have homicide departments instead of murder departments. Homicide is a crime in certain circumstances but not in others, when it's called justifiable homicide. Premeditated acts that, in legal terms, have been deemed justifiable homicide include the killing of a person in self-defense against a violent crime such as rape, the wartime killing of combatants who have not surrendered, and the government execution of a person who has received a death sentence. Determining what other acts constitute justifiable homicide is a murky proposition. Generally, any action one person takes to prevent a second person from violating or unlawfully killing a third can be justifiable.

MURDER

Murder is the **illegal killing** of one human being by another. It's a type of homicide and **a crime.** A key factor in murder is premeditation. This includes any advanced planning, whether it originated years or only seconds before the act. Though distinctions vary from state to state (see page 68), premeditated killing typically equates to first-degree murder. In some cases, murder has a legal defense, such as insanity or inability to differentiate right and wrong.

MANSLAUGHTER

Just as not all homicide is illegal, not all illegal killing is murder. The **unintentional—but still illegal—killing** of someone is called manslaughter. Besides being unpremeditated, manslaughter is also done without malice. Manslaughter is divided into two categories. Voluntary manslaughter includes killing when provoked. One example: someone lands a fatal punch in a spontaneous fight. Another: while in the midst of a felony, a burglar (see page 84) intercepted by a guard knocks him down, and the impact causes head injuries that lead to death. These are called crimes in the "heat of passion," the presumption being that the killer would normally not take such extreme action. Voluntary manslaughter can be deemed second-degree murder. Involuntary manslaughter is a killing due to recklessness. An example is killing a person by accidentally hitting him with a car. Manslaughter incurs less severe penalties than murder.

Homicide is the killing of another, whether lawful or unlawful, accidental or intentional, justifiable or unjustifiable. Both murder and manslaughter are types of homicide. Both are unlawful, but murder is intentional and often premeditated while manslaughter is negligent.

What's the difference between...
JUSTICE and REVENGE?

With which superhero defenders would you feel safer, the Justice League or the Revenge League? Your intellectual side may lean toward the former, your emotional the latter. With justice, there is some hope of rehabilitation. With revenge, not so much. Revenge is justice gone wild.

Marilyn vos Savant, resident genius columnist for *Parade* magazine, neatly summarizes the difference as follows: revenge feels right only to those involved, justice feels right even to outsiders. **Revenge is personal and justice is societal** or, some might even say, bureaucratic. While justice is about righteousness as determined by the majority, revenge is retaliation by an individual or group with little if any concern about what the community will think— or what society has made legal. That doesn't eliminate the possibility that revenge will be perceived as fair; it's just not validated in advance. Revenge can be undertaken **anonymously,** but justice, in order to serve the greater good, is usually delivered **out in the open.**

One implication of justice is that **punishment must fit the crime.** Revenge is not confined by the same guidelines. If someone dents your car, justice would prescribe that you seek to retrieve damages through socially acceptable channels such as filing an insurance claim. Revenge would urge you to grab a bat and smash the bad driver's car however you see fit. The notion of "an eye for an eye" is at least as old as the Bible. Both justice and revenge may be carried out with anger, but only revenge is fueled predominantly by it. People acting in the spirit of justice see it as a positive action. Revenge is more primal, and more likely to be viewed as negative.

To some, certain punishments sanctioned in the name of justice are as barbaric as those undertaken for revenge. The death penalty is an example. Supporters say that it is just. Opponents say that no form of retaliatory killing can be condoned.

Defenders of revenge may legitimize it by claiming that **extreme actions justify extreme reactions.** Others feel that revenge lowers the avenger to the level of the criminal, no matter how reprehensible the crime being avenged is. It can lead to a spiral of vengeful behavior, each action payback for the previous. In this sense, revenge can backfire and continue to hurt the avenger as well as the victim.

Ultimately, differentiating between justice and revenge is as simple or as complicated as defining good and evil, right and wrong. It just depends on whether you're the punisher or the punished.

What's the difference between...
PLEADING GUILTY and PLEADING NO CONTEST?

Guilty and no contest are separate paths that both lead to fines or convictions. In criminal cases, entering a plea of guilty is effectively the same as entering a plea of no contest. (On that note, entering a plea of no contest is exactly the same as entering a plea of *nolo contendere*, Latin for "I do not wish to argue.")

PLEADING GUILTY

A person charged with a crime who pleads not guilty is thereby requesting a trial, presumably confident that a jury will see his innocence. A person who pleads guilty is, obviously, **owning up to the offense** and prepared to face the consequences.

PLEADING NO CONTEST

A person who pleads no contest is **not admitting guilt–but not denying it, either.** And "no contest" doesn't mean "no punishment." That plea waives the right to trial by jury, but the court will still issue a sentence, and most likely will do so as if the defendant had pleaded guilty. After all, if someone doesn't defend himself against charges, regardless of the semantics, it still appears to be an admission of guilt.

Defendants plead no contest for a variety of reasons. It prevents a guilty verdict from being used against them if a civil suit is later filed. It bypasses both a trial in which they could be found guilty and the potential media frenzy that may accompany it. Also, it's possible that a defendant honestly doesn't remember or understand the circumstances that led to the charges.

Bombardment / Dodgeball

In most sports, you go after the ball. In these sports, the ball goes after you—specifically your head, if possible.

For roughly a third of the school-aged population, gym class is more dreaded than pop quizzes, school dances, and cafeteria sloppy joes combined. For almost all of that third, bombardment and dodgeball are the most dreaded of all gym class humiliation techniques. Many would even say they're precariously close to criminal (and some school districts have started to agree).

Both games involve using kickballs as missiles—if you're hit by a ball, you're out, and if you catch a ball, the thrower is out. The entire time, the level of panic is so high you're on the verge of soiling your unwashed gym shorts.

Though equal in their belligerence, bombardment and dodgeball are different in their styles of physical and mental terrorizing. Bombardment is like role-playing and the scene is a firing squad—two teams square off from opposite sides of the gym and can't cross the center line. Dodgeball is also like role-playing, only the scene is a bunch of sailors who abandoned a sinking ship and are surrounded by sharks—a circle of ball-throwers simply picks off a hapless group in the middle one by one.

In bombardment, the frantic participants are facing all their opponents, while in dodge-ball, they have their backs to some of their opponents. On the downside, this means dodgeball victims have a greater chance of being pegged by the kickball since there's less room to flee. On the upside, there's also a greater chance that they'll get hit in the back of the head instead of the face.

What's the difference?

RELIGION

JESUS and CHRIST

REVEREND, PRIEST, MINISTER, PASTOR, and PREACHER

SATAN, THE DEVIL, BEELZEBUB, and LUCIFER

What's the difference between...
JESUS and CHRIST?

Christ was not Jesus's last name any more than *H* was his middle initial.

JESUS

Jesus was the **name of an influential teacher** who, to Christians, was the Son of God whose beliefs form the basis of Christianity. The name is the Greek form of "Joshua," which means "the Lord saves." Jesus lived in the first century C.E., a time when names referenced where a person was from—hence, Jesus of Nazareth. Names were also formed based on who a person's father was, so Jesus could have been called Jesus, son of Joseph. He was not called Jesus Christ in his lifetime, but he did call himself both Son of Man and Son of God. The Gospels include other titles for him, including Prophet and King of the Jews.

CHRIST

Christ was a **title for this man,** from the Greek (via Latin) for "anointed one" and equivalent to the Hebrew term *Messiah*. Therefore, "Jesus Christ" can be translated as "the Lord saves the anointed one." The term *Christ* can be prefaced by *the*. It can also refer to others, those who've had the Holy Spirit poured on them at a baptism. Jews don't believe that Jesus was divine, and they don't claim to know who the Messiah will be. Christians believe that Jesus is the Christ who died for the sins of humanity and who will return as the Messiah, bringing world peace.

Irresistible Force / Immovable Object

When it comes to title bouts, this one is so big that some people can't get their minds around it. And it's not available on pay-per-view. It may seem like this classic confrontation would have to end in a stalemate, but here's the thing: in the real world, someone (or something) always wins.

If two entities of such power ever do show up and clash, you can be sure they're not going to fight to a tie, then shake hands and grab a beer. Beings capable of such might also don't give up or play nice. This means that there is a difference.

But it's tough to figure out what that is since this head-to-head currently exists only in science fiction. So here's some conjecture. An irresistible force is in motion. An immovable object is, well, not moving. Alternately, an irresistible force may involve Krazy Glue, duct tape, or perhaps Velcro. No, scratch that—an immovable object could involve the same. Lastly, an irresistible force sounds sexier. An immovable object seems like it would be pudgy.

What's the difference between...
a REVEREND, a PRIEST, a MINISTER, a PASTOR, and a PREACHER?

These are but five of the dozens of roles or titles the men and women of the modern clergy can have. But since God is our witness, not our editor, we don't have the room to address deacon, bishop, parson, chaplain, rector, vicar, and the rest here. Suffice it to say that they've all got the home number of some form of Holiness.

REVEREND

Reverend is a somewhat **generic yet deferential prefix for a Christian leader.** Unlike many other religious titles, it has no biblical reference. Members of the media sometimes use it as a catchall when referring to any number of types of ordained leaders, regardless of the actual titles their churches use for them. Some clergy discourage use of the title *Reverend* because they feel that humans should revere Jesus (see page 94), not other humans—not even those who've dedicated their lives to his mission. *Reverend* is properly used as an adjective before a person's name rather than as a noun. You would not call William Rogers a reverend; you would say "the Reverend William Rogers."

PRIEST

A priest is an **officiant of a church who has authority to perform rites.** Throughout the centuries, numerous religions (many of them non-Christian) used the term, which was often applied to a figure who conducted rituals of sacrifice. Today, the term is predominant in Roman Catholicism, Eastern Orthodoxy, and several other branches of Christianity.

MINISTER

A minister is commonly a person who **leads the congregation of a Protestant church.** Some Protestants prefer *minister* to *priest* because of the historical association of priests with sacrifice. A minister is seen as someone who is sometimes set apart from laypeople while at other times one of the people.

PASTOR

Pastor is **another word for priest or minister,** also common among Protestants, including Baptists and Lutherans. At times the word refers to a person who provides spiritual **counsel,** not necessarily a person who conducts services. It comes from the Latin term for "shepherd." Some Protestants use "pastor" in direct address.

PREACHER

A preacher is typically **a person who proclaims rather than develops gospel.** The word is less about guiding a congregation and more about informing them (or reminding them) of the teachings the Christian church holds as important. People who view preaching as trying to force others how to think sometimes use *preacher* in a derogatory way. On occasion, *preacher* is used as a synonym for *pastor,* though technically a preacher has separate functions from this and the other positions described here.

What's the difference between…
SATAN, THE DEVIL, BEELZEBUB, and LUCIFER?

There's a dude (or supreme being, if you're picky) who's such bad news that no one name is enough to identify him. The material written to define and delineate his crop of names is so dense with pagan, biblical, apocryphal, and medieval interpretations it can make your head spin (as can demonic possession, apparently). All are intertwined and all have evil connotations today, though not all started out that way.

SATAN

Satan, the term that most often encompasses these others, is the **name of God's archenemy** in Judaism and Christianity. In Jewish tradition, God did not create this evil being; in Christian tradition, God did. The word frequently means "accuser." Satan turns up in different roles in the Bible—early on, he even works for God. Though some interpret the serpent in the Garden of Eden as a guise of Satan, many scholars take it for what it is, just another talking reptile (see page 22). In the Book of Job in the Old Testament, *Satan* is his title, not a proper name, and he doesn't resemble later incarnations. He's something like an angelic prosecuting attorney for God, roaming the land and looking for people who have been sinful (again, he's

an "accuser"). The Old Testament doesn't mention the fall from heaven. In the New Testament, post-fall and proper name now instated, he tries to tempt Jesus (see page 94) into worshiping him and cements his reputation as the personification of evil. *Satan* comes with a stack of synonyms from numerous sources, including the Prince of one of three D's: Devils, Demons, or Darkness. Just as his names and roles have differed over the years, so has his appearance. Today, a default depiction is a satyr-like creature with a pointed beard and a pitchfork, though he's not described this way in the Bible. He's also creeped people out as an angel with batlike wings or just a dapper man with a glint of wickedness in his eyes.

THE DEVIL

The Devil (sometimes lowercased), the only one of these terms that gets a *the,* is regarded in the Judeo-Christian scheme as a **fallen angel.** However, the Devil takes various forms in many world religions, and his evil quotient is varied. According to Christianity, the Devil tries to lead humans astray from the path toward redemption. The word *devil* has been used as a translation for the Hebrew word *Satan.* It pops up more often than "Satan" in the New Testament. As such, they share several other meanings in addition to ones already mentioned, including "adversary" and "slanderer."

BEELZEBUB

Beelzebub first appears in the Old Testament as a **Philistine god in the city of Ekron,** southwest of Jerusalem. In Hebrew, the word means "lord of the flies" (and yes, that's where the title of the 1954 William Golding novel comes from). By the New Testament, he has in effect merged with the concept of Satan and evolved into the aforementioned Prince of Devils or Prince of Demons (sometimes these phrases are not capitalized). By the time of John Milton's epic poem *Paradise Lost* (1667), he seems to have been demoted, as there he's the fallen angel second-in-command to Satan. Today, *Beelzebub* is often used interchangeably with *Satan* or *the Devil.*

LUCIFER

The term *Lucifer* is from the Latin for "light bearer" or "morning star"—hardly sinister sounding. When the Bible was being translated into Latin, early Christians interpreted a passage from Babylonian cuneiform mentioning "Lucifer" as the story of Satan—an angel in high standing who rebelled against God and was tossed from heaven to hell, where he became the **leader of the demons.** In *Paradise Lost*, Satan was originally called Lucifer. Today, the term is used as a synonym for *Satan* or *the Devil.*

What's the difference?

MYTH AND SCIENCE FICTION

APPARITION, GHOST, SPIRIT, and POLTERGEIST

EGYPTIAN SPHINX and GREEK SPHINX

FABLE and FAIRY TALE

ROBOT and ANDROID

WEREWOLF and WOLF MAN

What's the difference between…
an APPARITION, a SPIRIT, a GHOST, and a POLTERGEIST?

There sure are a lot of words for related beings that most people never encounter—and that many don't even believe in. Since no one we know of has interviewed any of these supernatural forces, none of the following definitions is set in stone.

APPARITION

Apparition is a **general term for any manifestation of a deceased person** that can appear to the living in a form similar to the one it had when it was alive. Adding more "eep" to "creepy," sometimes an apparition can be of a living person who is far away at the time. Among parapsychologists, *apparition* is often the preferred term for what the rest of us simply call a ghost.

SPIRIT

A spirit is sometimes considered the same as a soul, the **essence of a living thing** that remains after the physical body has passed on. The term has a less unnerving connotation than *ghost*. While ghosts have been characterized as beings trapped between life and death, spirits are often described as having **"crossed over"** completely. Therefore, they may be appearing to the living by choice and in a state of peace, not due to confusion over their situation. Some people make a distinction that ghosts can't communicate with the living while spirits can.

GHOST

A ghost is the **intangible energy of a deceased entity** that can be seen, smelled, felt, or sometimes heard. Many are of an organic nature, though ghosts of inanimate objects like ships have also been reported. Often ghosts appear merely as orbs or streaks of light, but sometimes they're humanlike and dressed as they did in life—only now they're transparent, misty, and maybe only partially visible. Some ghosts seem to be aware of the living and may try to interact with them. Others seem more like perpetually replaying "recordings" of some activity a deceased person did before his death, such as washing dishes; those ghosts don't notice their surroundings.

People who "feel" ghosts describe sudden sensations of hot, cold, or wind—or just detect that they're not alone anymore. Ghosts are considered "earthbound"—trapped in a location that they had a connection to when they were alive. People have floated numerous theories to explain why that might be: ghosts are saddled with unfinished business, they died violently or accidentally, they're out to punish someone, or they want to watch over loved ones. They **recur until their goal is accomplished,** which gives rise to the concept of a haunting, even though a ghost may not be trying to intentionally scare anyone. Some believe that ghosts don't even realize they're ghosts.

POLTERGEIST

A poltergeist ("noisy ghost" in German) is a paranormal disturbance that is typically heard but not seen. Of all these paranormal categories, poltergeists can have the most pronounced effect on the physical world. Their tactics can include rapping on walls, moving furniture, or even touching a person. Poltergeist activity is perceived as hostile, and over time can escalate to a dangerous level. Some parapsy-

chologists postulate that poltergeists aren't aspects of once-living things but rather **energy masses that can be generated unknowingly by the thoughts of a living person,** particularly a stressed-out teenager. (Think twice before grounding your teen.) In that sense, the poltergeist phenomenon may actually be a form of psychokinesis, the ability to move objects with the mind.

What's the difference between...
an EGYPTIAN SPHINX and the GREEK SPHINX?

Other than their native tongue, of course…

EGYPTIAN SPHINX

The Egyptian sphinx was a creature commonly composed of a **man's head and a lion's body** and portrayed in the recumbent position. The face was usually modeled after whichever pharaoh ordered that sphinx's construction. Some sphinxes had the head of a ram or a hawk (though, presumably, no pharaohs did).

Our familiarity with Egyptian sphinxes comes largely from statues. The sphinx was a **recurring motif,** often "guarding" temples, tombs, and other sacred sites.

GREEK SPHINX

The Greek Sphinx was a creature of myth (see page 107) with the **head and chest of a woman, the body of a lion, and wings.** Sometimes she also sported a snakelike tail. She's often depicted seated, not lying, her size no larger than an average lion.

There was **only one** Greek Sphinx. No ancient statues of the Greek Sphinx are known to exist; we've learned of her predominantly from writings. She first appeared in Greek culture around 1600 B.C.E.

The most famous Egyptian sphinx is the Great Sphinx of Giza, a colossal statue and the only one of the Seven Ancient Wonders of the World still standing (rather, lying) today. It is believed to bear the now weather-beaten mug of the pharaoh Khafre (also known as Chephren). Customarily, the Great Sphinx is dated to about 2600 B.C.E., though some think it may be even older. Historians don't know what the Egyptians initially called sphinxes, as the word comes from Greek usage.

According to the myth that took root hundreds of years later, the Sphinx was stationed on a large rock outside the city of Thebes, where her job was to challenge passersby with a riddle. If a person solved it, he could continue on his way. If not, she strangled or devoured him. Here's one translation of her riddle (but if you don't figure it out, no worries, you won't meet a grisly end!): "What animal goes on four legs in the morning, two at noon, and three in the evening?" Oedipus, who would eventually get stuck in even ickier situations, solved the rid-dle: man, who crawls on all fours as a baby, walks upright though midlife, and uses a cane in old age. Enraged (she was used to winning), the Sphinx hurled herself to the ground—and her death. The word *sphinx* comes from the Greek *sphingo* ("to strangle") or *sphingein* ("to bind tight").

What's the difference between...
a FABLE and a FAIRY TALE?

Think Aesop versus the Brothers Grimm. The forms of storytelling these guys typify are separated by more than just a couple thousand years, but definitions of these terms are mercurial and do overlap in ways.

FABLE	FAIRY TALE
A fable is a **short instructional tale,** typically featuring **animals with human traits** as the central characters and taking place at an unspecified time and place. Fables are fictitious and don't pretend to be otherwise.	A fairy tale is a fictional story involving fanciful characters and settings and **told as amusement.** Fairies need not be involved, but fairy tales are **populated by imaginary figures** such as goblins, giants, witches, and assorted others. The primary audience for fairy tales is children, though some do include grotesque violence. A customary—but not mandatory—opening for fairy tales is "Once upon a time…"
Each fable is constructed to deliver a moral (see page 66), often explicitly. When done reading, you should be **clear on how to behave.**	Fairy tales may contain an embedded lesson, but unlike fables they **don't spell it out.**
Well-known fables include "The Boy Who Cried Wolf" and "The Tortoise and the Hare."	"Jack and the Beanstalk" and "Cinderella" are two examples of fairy tales.

RELATED TERMS: *A* **myth** *is a story with supernatural elements set in a time that is usually not firmly dated, though it may resemble a real past era. Myths frequently explain the origins of natural phenomenon, places, traditions, and so on. Many myths are presented as potentially true, though the full extent of that truth might never be verified. Some consider the Loch Ness Monster a myth that one day may turn out to be a real animal.*

A **legend** *is a traditional story that has some historical basis, if only vaguely. They are easily confused with myths, though legends may not seem as far-fetched. Examples include the accounts of King Arthur or Robin Hood.*

A **folktale** *is a story told to entertain, often delivered orally. Some folktales are exaggerations based on real people (Johnny Appleseed) and some are just plain exaggerations (Paul Bunyan). Many folktales reference a specific culture.*

A **parable** *is a brief, allegorical narrative presented as if it could have actually occurred. Parables are sometimes religious in nature. Their point is to illustrate proper conduct. In being didactic, they're cousins of fables, but they usually feature more realistic characters.*

Jack (Who Climbed a Beanstalk)/Jack (Who Hung with Jill)/Jack (Who Was Nimble)/Jack Sprat/Little Jack Horner/Jack (Who Built a House)

Nursery rhymes are stocked with more jacks than a playing cards factory. These six are the most well known. Despite the rumors, they are not all the same guy at different stages in life. The truth is that they were brothers—illegitimate sextuplets of the Old Woman Who Lived in a Shoe. She had so many children that she sent six to other rhymes and cut all ties. But why did she name them all Jack? Again, she lived in a shoe. The lady wasn't exactly sane.

What's the difference between...
a ROBOT and an ANDROID?

This one is not just for geeks (see page 30) and nerds (ditto). Science fiction writers, scientists, engineers, and probably legislators also discuss the various forms of artificial intelligence and the implications of their development. The distinctions vary among sources and may change as technology evolves. As robots and androids inch closer to an eerie level of sentience, *they* may begin debating similar questions—such as "What's the difference between a human and a clone?"

ROBOT

A robot is a **fully mechanical, conscienceless device** programmed to perform certain tasks. Some act on command while others are on automatic.

Though made of metal or plastic, they **may resemble humans,** but that is not an indispensable part of the definition. Robots can be clunky 1950s sci-fi cylinders with eyes and droning voices, automated "arms"

ANDROID

An android is an **autonomous, humanlike robot.** Androids are often described as partially mechanical and partially biological; sometimes they are described as fully organic, yet still artificially made.

While their insides are robotic, their surface is covered with synthetic skin and features. This can make them **indistinguishable from a real person at first glance;** they are sometimes called humanoids. In science

RELATED TERM: *A cyborg is a human who has received mechanical implants that he controls with his brain. The term stands for "cybernetic organism." Though cyborgs comprise both living tissue and metal circuitry, as androids typically do, they start as human and merge with machine, whereas androids are not built on an existing biological frame. Like the Six Million Dollar Man of 1970s TV fame, cyborgs are capable of superhuman feats.*

helping to build other machines on an assembly line, or tiny spy gadgets, or they can take any number of other forms. Even if they look like a person, it is usually clear from their movements that robots are not human.

Robots of the nonhumanlike variety are **already at work** in the world today, often being used to replace human effort in repetitive labor.

fiction, they can be programmed with a conscience, but they may not experience emotions, and they don't need water, food, or sleep. Androids are also robots but robots are not necessarily androids.

Sophisticated androids **don't exist** beyond the pages of fiction…yet.

What's the difference between...
a WEREWOLF and a WOLF MAN?

From a universal perspective, a human who changes into a wolf and back again is a werewolf. From a Universal (as in Studios) perspective, a human who can transform into a hirsute human with big teeth is a wolf man.

WEREWOLF

Werewolves have prowled the moon-bathed nights of many world-wide cultures in history, notably in Europe. A werewolf is a cursed being, a **human bitten by a supernatural wolf creature** who can then **shapeshift into a wolf himself**—an actual, four-legged wolf.

WOLF MAN

In 1941, Universal released *The Wolf Man*, a horror film starring Lon Chaney Jr. as the titular beast. Two earlier films had the same or nearly the same title, but neither achieved classic status nor modified werewolf folklore like the 1941 version did. Chaney's character is **bitten by a wolf that turns out to be a werewolf.** However, that causes him to transform into not another wolf or werewolf but rather a **hairy, upright humanoid with fangs.** Though he doesn't resemble his fully animal "foreweres" of many a lycanthropic legend (see page 107), other characters—seemingly unaware of their vehicle's title—refer to Chaney's alter ego as a werewolf, not a wolf man. The film seems to imply that this is because they perceive him to be a pure wolf...a wolf that wears clothes, walks on two feet, and leaves nonpawlike footprints. This is where the "man" part comes in—if not for the characters, then at least for the marketing (see page 166) monsters at Universal.

RELATED TERM: Lycanthropy *is the psychiatric condition in which a person believes he is or can turn into a wolf.* Lycanthrope *is Greek for "wolf man."*

There was a time when a movie would come out, tell its story, and leave it at that. Now even the dopiest movies are packaged in a couple of versions minimum, notably the one seen in theaters and the "special" director's cut available later on DVD. On a side note, if that's the director's cut, who directed what was in the cinema? And shouldn't "cut" imply "shorter," not "bloated with an extra two hours of footage"?

The difference is elementary. Even if a film was good in theaters, the director's cut pads it beyond the patience of anyone other than a film buff. And if a film was bad in theaters, the director's cut renders it unwatchable.

What's the difference?

NATURE, WEATHER, AND SPACE

CYCLONE, HURRICANE, TYPHOON, and TORNADO

LAKE AND POND

METEOROID, METEOR, and METEORITE

MOLD and MILDEW

PARTLY CLOUDY and PARTLY SUNNY

SOLSTICE and EQUINOX

STREAM, CREEK, and BROOK

TIDAL WAVE and TSUNAMI

WINTER STORM WATCH, WINTER WEATHER ADVISORY, and WINTER STORM WARNING

What's the difference between...
a CYCLONE, a HURRICANE, a TYPHOON, and a TORNADO?

They're already the fiercest storms on Earth, and if we continue to get them mixed up it may make them even angrier.

CYCLONE

Cyclone is a general term for **all classes of circular storms** composed of winds that swirl around a center of low pressure. Contrary to what the movie version of *The Wizard of Oz* has implanted in the collective mind, *cyclone* is not merely a synonym for *tornado*. Since there are many types of cyclones, precise weather forecasters use the word with a qualifier. Unmodified, the word is often used to categorize storms **in and around the Indian Ocean.**

HURRICANE

A hurricane (also called a "tropical cyclone") is a large weather system that brings **heavy rain and sustained winds** of seventy-four miles (119 km) per hour or greater in the **North Atlantic Ocean, Caribbean Sea, Gulf of Mexico, and eastern North Pacific Ocean.** Hurricanes and tropical storms in general are fueled by air heated by the warm sea. If they hit land, they typically peter out—though sometimes only after causing extensive damage. Hurricane season is June to November, peaking in September. Hurricanes are often more than a hundred miles (161 km) wide and have featured winds that have been recorded at speeds of up to 190 miles (306 km) per hour. On average, hurricanes last about a week.

RELATED TERMS: *In the United States,* **twister** *is a slang word for tornado.*

A **funnel cloud** *is a cone-shaped storm that appears to be hanging down from a cloud, but unlike a tornado it doesn't touch the surface of the Earth.*

A **monsoon** *is a wind that changes direction with the seasons and often brings heavy rain. It is largely associated with Asia, though monsoons do happen elsewhere.*

TYPHOON

A typhoon is essentially **the same as a hurricane, except for location.** It occurs in the **western North Pacific Ocean.** Also, typhoons can be stronger than hurricanes because the ocean water is warmer where they occur. Typhoon season is May to December, though typhoons could happen at any time during the year.

TORNADO

A tornado is a **spinning column of air** descending from a cloud to the ground. Though they can occur worldwide, they're most frequent on the **plains of the United States.** Compared to tropical cyclones, tornadoes are small, but still extremely dangerous. Tornadoes are on average four hundred to five hundred feet (122 to 152 m) wide. They travel twenty to fifty miles (32 to 80 km) per hour and churn at speeds of up to 250 miles (402 km) per hour. Tornadoes typically last from a few minutes to an hour at most.

Cyclones hit most commonly in the Indian Ocean, hurricanes in the Atlantic, typhoons in the Pacific, and tornadoes on land. And hopefully not when you're around.

What's the difference between...
a LAKE and a POND?

No official parameters of these geographic terms exist, but a few (debatable) differences emerge if you dip deep enough. Your guess is probably that a lake is larger than a pond. While many agree, exceptions are everywhere people skinny-dip and ice fish (simultaneously or not). In the end, perhaps the most viable difference is not size but ecology—though the ecology is frequently determined by the size.

LAKE	POND
A lake is a natural body of water surrounded by land. Many are fresh water, but a manmade reservoir or recreational destination can also be called a lake. Lakes are often expansive enough to have **currents or waves.**	A pond is a natural body of water surrounded by land. Wait—that sounds familiar. We could rephrase the definition as "a body of water surrounded by land and smaller than a lake." But it may not be easy to ascertain whether this is accurate the majority of the time. And how small? One source says small enough that you wouldn't need a boat to cross it. Ponds are **still bodies of water;** the only movement on the surface comes from the occasional creature peeking out or a breeze skimming across the water.
Some lakes are deep enough to have **more than one temperature layer** in the summer, the top being the warmest. In deeper lakes where light can't penetrate to the bottom, many if not most of the living things that call it home stay closer to the surface.	If they are indeed small, ponds have a fairly **consistent water temperature** from top to bottom. Ponds are often thick with rooted plants and coated with scum, a film of decaying vegetation.

"Lake" and "pond" have a linguistic difference that may be as valid as any other: "lake" works either before or after a name (Lake Superior, Crater Lake), while "pond" always seems to bring up the rear (Kettle Pond, Trap Pond).

Human/Plant

Both need sunlight and water to grow. Both have roots. Neither are minerals. Neither has a large representation in Antarctica. As for the differences, they're strangely opposite, even though the average person and the average plant may not seem so different on the surface.

In plants, brown means sickness (exhibit A: wilted deli lettuce) and green means health (as in bursting with yummy chlorophyll). Meanwhile, in humans, brown means health (at least people *think* a rich, nutty tan looks healthier than pale skin) and green means sickness (as in the color of skin before upchucking).

What's the difference between…
a METEOROID, a METEOR, and a METEORITE?

Taking it from the top (space) to the bottom (the ground), one chunk of stone can transform from meteoroid to meteor to meteorite just by falling.

METEOROID

Look up in the sky. No, higher up. Higher…stop when you reach outer space. A rocky or metallic **fragment floating through the darkness of space** is a meteoroid. They can be as wee as a speck of sand or almost a kilometer across, though most are smaller than pebbles. Meteoroids are often pieces that have broken off from asteroids, comets, or other cosmic bodies.

METEOR

Look up in the sky again. Not that high this time. Yes, that's just right. An **arc of light plummeting toward Earth** is a meteor, sometimes called a shooting star. Meteors occur when the lumps formerly known as meteoroids rocket out of space into Earth's atmosphere. Technically, the meteor is the streak of light, not the solid object, but now many refer to the rock itself as a meteor, too. When multiple meteoroids cross into Earth's orbit at once, it's called a meteor shower or, if it's especially intense, a meteor storm. Either way, don't bother with an umbrella.

METEORITE

Look down. You just may be treading on a celestial expatriate. A **meteor that reaches the planet** is a meteorite. Brave as these space rocks may be to try to make it to Earth (if they could talk, they might say, "Meteor not, here I come!"), not all do. Many get so hot as they accelerate through the atmosphere that they vaporize. As with meteoroids, meteorite sizes can vary from teeny-tiny to crater-causing. Big meteoroids stand a greater chance of surviving the extreme friction of falling and landing. According to one estimate, only about five hundred fist-sized meteorites slam into Earth every year. Almost no incidents of people being struck by meteorites are on record.

RELATED TERMS: *Aspiring space travelers who never got further than driving a Saturn may also be curious as to how asteroids and comets compare to the triple* m's.

Asteroids *are masses of rock or metal that travel in a belt around the sun. They are smaller than planets but bigger than meteoroids. The biggest one known, Ceres, is 580 miles (933 km) in diameter, though the average asteroid diameter is less than 62 miles (100 km).*

Comets *are balls of ice and rock that zip around the edges of the solar system, often with a visible tail of gas and dust.*

What's the difference between…
MOLD and MILDEW?

Would you believe that disinfectant companies made up one of these terms in an attempt to sell twice as many products? Of course you would—but it's not true.

MOLD

Mold is a simple living organism that can develop with the right combination of warmth, moisture, and nutrients. Along with mushrooms and yeast, it is a **type of fungus.** It can grow on organic matter, clothing, leather, and paper, as well as ceilings, walls, and floors. It is perhaps most commonly associated with spoiled food such as bread or cream cheese.

Mold is microscopic but becomes visible as it multiplies, alarming its discoverer with its expanding, fuzzy patch of threads. It can be a shade of white, gray, green, or, most often, black. Its musty odor can show up before you see the first sign of fuzz. Though certain molds can cause disease, others use their powers for good, contributing to products as disconnected as cheese and penicillin.

MILDEW

Mildew is also a growth fitting that description. Some sources claim that mildew is simply the class of mold that grows on fabrics. Others define mildew as powdery mold that grows specifically on plants, including edibles such as cucumbers and grapes.

Still others use "mildew" to describe the discoloration that mold causes. Finally, some reserve the word for only white formations of mold, lumping all other colors under "mold." But by most accounts, mold and mildew are unpleasantly the same.

What's the difference between…
PARTLY CLOUDY and PARTLY SUNNY?

The answer is mostly clear: they are the same, except that one doesn't exist. Technically, the correct phrase is *partly cloudy*. The Weather Channel's online glossary does not even have an entry for "partly sunny."

PARTLY CLOUDY

Leave it to the National Weather Service, a government operation, to choose the gloomier of the two as the official phrase. As with most bureaucratic designations, "partly cloudy" has **numbers attached.** The NWS divides the blue-if-we're-lucky above us into eight sections; the number of sections occupied by clouds determines the forecast.

Kind of Day	Cloud Cover
"Partly cloudy" *(that is, "partly sunny")*	$3/8$ to $5/8$
"Mostly cloudy"	$6/8$ to $7/8$
"Cloudy"	$8/8$

PARTLY SUNNY

Many meteorologists say "partly sunny" to be **optimistic,** or possibly because they don't know it's no more legitimate than "wholly moony." Some prefer to use "partly sunny" in the only period it could be applicable—that is, during the day—while reserving "partly cloudy" exclusively for nighttime use.

RELATED TERMS: *Some regions are large enough that the cloud cover is not the same from one end to the other. That's why you'll sometimes hear descriptions such as "mixture of sun and clouds" or "variable cloudiness."*

What's the difference between...
a SOLSTICE and an EQUINOX?

The Earth is a master multitasker; it orbits the sun and rotates on its axis at the same time. The axis is tilted at a 23.5-degree angle; it's this tilting that causes the change of seasons across most of the globe. The days that start each season are either solstices or equinoxes. These astronomical terms concern the direction the Earth is tilting in relation to the sun at those four moments during the year. In the Northern Hemisphere, June and December sport a solstice each, and the vernal and autumnal equinoxes occur in March and September, respectively. Remember that the seasons are reversed in the Southern Hemisphere, so if you're there, just hold this book upside down.

SOLSTICE

The **summer solstice** falls on or around June 21—the longest day of the year in the Northern Hemisphere, meaning the day with the **most hours of daylight** (more than twelve). On that day, the North Pole is tilted toward the sun while the South Pole aims away from it. At the Arctic Circle, it's the only day of the year in which the sun stays above the horizon for twenty-four hours. Meanwhile, at the Antarctic Circle, it's the only day of the year in which the sun doesn't rise above the horizon for twenty-four hours. Good day to sleep in.

The **winter solstice** falls on or around December 21, a bleak day in the Northern Hemisphere if for no other reason than it's the day with the **fewest hours of daylight** of the year (less than twelve). On that day, the North Pole is angled away from the sun while the South Pole tilts toward it. At the Arctic Circle, it's the only day of the year in which the sun doesn't rise above the horizon for twenty-four hours. Meanwhile, at the Antarctic Circle, it's the only day of the year in which the sun stays above the horizon for twenty-four hours.

Two superlatives are enough for the solstices: they are the longest and shortest days of the year, but not the warmest or coolest.

EQUINOX

The **vernal equinox** falls on or around March 21 and heralds the beginning of spring, though not as melodically as robins. The **autumnal equinox** falls on or around September 22 and kicks off autumn, which means that kids are routinely being duped into starting school three weeks before summer officially ends.

On both equinoxes, neither the North nor the South Pole is tilted toward—or away—from the sun. Each pole is still maintaining its standard tilt, but they're pointing toward another spot in space. This means a **twelve-hour day almost everywhere** on the planet.

What's the difference between...
a STREAM, a CREEK, and a BROOK?

If a river were Donald Duck, stream, creek, and brook would be Huey, Dewey, and Louie. They're all natural, "nephew-sized" courses of water. As with many other geographic terms, the definitions seem to revolve around size, but exceptions run wild.

STREAM

A stream is a general term for a body of flowing fresh water, usually **smaller than a river.** Streams can be further classified depending on when they are active (intermittent streams run only part of the year, while perennial streams are year-round) and where the water comes from and goes to (gaining streams take in water from underground pockets, while losing streams leak water into those underground pockets).

CREEK

A creek is a current of water that is normally **smaller than a stream but larger than a brook.** Creeks can also be tidal. *Creek* is a common term in the northern United States, though it does turn up elsewhere, too. In fact, its usage can vary depending on location within the United States. In arid areas, a creek may be known as a river (bypassing stream altogether).

BROOK

A brook is a current of water that is **smaller than a stream or creek** and sometimes trickling between two other flows of water. Brooks often form from water seeping up from the ground or from substantial rainfall. The term is in wide use in the northeastern, coastal United States. Some brooks (and some creeks, for that matter) are small enough for a person to wade through, or even just step over.

What's the difference between...
a TIDAL WAVE and a TSUNAMI?

Tsunami is Japanese for "harbor wave." At first that may seem like a clue as to what distinguishes it from a tidal wave, but tsunamis don't happen exclusively in harbors. Both tidal waves and tsunamis are destructive water phenomena, but their origins are different.

TIDAL WAVE

A tidal wave is a swell of cresting water **caused by the gravitational effect of the moon,** sometimes amplified by strong winds. *Tidal wave* appears to mean both the standard rise of water and also an atypically large rise. To purists, it can't just mean any water situation that is unconnected to the tide. A tidal wave is a **"surface" ripple,** usually not affecting water deeper than thirty feet (9 m).

TSUNAMI

A tsunami is a series of ocean waves **triggered by an earthquake, a landslide, a volcanic eruption, or even a meteorite** (see page 119). From shore, an approaching tsunami can resemble a rapidly rising tide, and the degree of devastation it brings is partially determined by the tide level at the time it hits—but a tsunami is not caused by tides. The mass of water displaced by the generating event typically **extends from the surface all the way to the ocean floor.** The distance between waves is usually between 60 and 120 miles (97 to 193 km) (it can take between five minutes to more than an hour for successive waves to pass the same point), but the height of each wave is only about one to two feet (30 to 60 cm). These factors make a tsunami imperceptible on open sea; the threat becomes apparent only as it nears a coast. Then separate tsunami waves "bunch up" into one massive wall of water that can reach heights of one hundred feet (30 m). And it travels faster than a human can run.

What's the difference between...
a WINTER STORM WATCH, a WINTER WEATHER ADVISORY, and a WINTER STORM WARNING?

If you live below the snowline and don't know these terms, just kick back in your capris, sip your tropical drink, and scoff at the masochistic northerners. Unless, of course, you need to seek shelter from an approaching hurricane (see page 114). The National Weather Service developed a system of alerts to inform the public as to just how intense the next mess will be, though the specifics (snow or sleet or rain and how much) depend on the region. If you do live in a snow zone, you hear these terms every winter—and it seems like you're shoveling after every mention. Wherever you are, here's the lowdown on this lingo.

WINTER STORM WATCH

A Winter Storm Watch indicates that there is a **threat of severe weather,** though not a certainty. Typically, the NWS issues a watch twelve to thirty-six hours in advance. It carries with it the potential for heavy snow or considerable ice accumulation. A watch asks residents to be prepared to take action, not to take immediate action.

The names of these bugs invoke two of the most formidable forces of nature. The bugs, however, are pussycats. Fireflies don't breathe fire and lightning bugs don't shoot lightning bolts from their eyes, so there goes your first guess. Reverse entomology won't work either, as fireflies can't shoot lightning bolts and lightning bugs can't breathe fire. If they're named literally, fireflies glow steadily for a while but will either die down or spread madly when left unattended, while lightning bugs flash their taillights for only a few seconds, usually just before thunder booms, and never in the same place twice.

WINTER WEATHER ADVISORY

A Winter Weather Advisory is issued once the **snow or sleet is in progress,** but it indicates an **inconvenience, not a danger to life or property**—yet. Slick streets (see page 139), patchy fog conditions, blowing snow, or other impediments to driving would result in an advisory. Don't freak out—but don't travel, either.

WINTER STORM WARNING

A Winter Storm Warning means freak out. Or at least take action to safeguard health and home from **hazardous conditions** already in progress. The NWS issues a warning when inclement weather seems likely to dump **seven or more inches (18 or more cm) of snow** within a twenty-four-hour period. When possible, warnings are dispatched twelve to twenty-four hours before the storm hits.

What's the difference?

GEOGRAPHY AND TRAVEL

EMBASSY, CONSULATE, and MISSION

ENGLAND, GREAT BRITAIN, THE UNITED KINGDOM,
and THE BRITISH ISLES

HIGHWAY, FREEWAY, EXPRESSWAY, and PARKWAY

THE NETHERLANDS and HOLLAND

ROAD, STREET, BOULEVARD, LANE, and AVENUE

What's the difference between...
an EMBASSY, a CONSULATE, and a MISSION?

On vacation on the far side of the globe, you realize only after you get to the hotel that you picked up the wrong suitcase at the airport. You open it and discover classified government information, a loaded gun, and bundles of cash. Before shock can set in, there's a bang at the door. Then there's the shock. Suddenly you're entangled in international intrigue and you didn't even have time to freshen up. You need to get the nearest piece of home, and you have no time for mistakes. Which building to run to? Here's your guide.

EMBASSY

An embassy is the **official representation of one nation situated within another,** typically in the capital city. The head of an embassy is an ambassador. Though the building in which this group operates is usually called the embassy, that word actually refers to the delegation itself; the building is properly known as a chancellery or chancery. Embassies engage in diplomatic relations with foreign governments and serve as spokespeople for their home nations. Another term used to refer to an embassy is *diplomatic mission.*

CONSULATE

A consulate is essentially a **junior embassy.** The senior official of a consulate is a consul. Any given country has only one embassy in another but can have multiple consulates, usually located in the larger cities. Consulates are resources for businesses and individuals, established to promote commercial growth and handle administrative duties such as issuing passports and visas. Unless you're a queen or prime minister, you'll be sorting out any and all relevant affairs in a consulate, not an embassy. If one country does not recognize the sovereignty of another, to show disapproval it may have a consulate (to help tourists and expatriates) but not an embassy there.

MISSION

Missions to the **United Nations** are known as permanent missions. While an embassy fosters harmony between its home and host nations and a consulate provides services to nationals, a permanent mission **fosters harmony between its home nation and all other member nations.** Permanent missions have also been set up in Geneva and other cities that are home to intergovernmental organizations.

What's the difference between...
ENGLAND, GREAT BRITAIN, the UNITED KINGDOM, and the BRITISH ISLES?

Remembering all fifty states (see page 68) may seem easier than distinguishing between these four European entities. But it's really just a matter of little fish, bigger fish, still bigger fish, and biggest fish.

Technically, **England is not a country.** Neither are Scotland and Wales, though all three are often described as such. England and Scotland are **kingdoms** (which sounds cooler than "country" anyway), and Wales is a principality (which, sorry to say, sounds lamer).

England, Scotland, and Wales occupy **Great Britain, the largest island** in Europe. Add Northern Ireland to the mix and you've got the **United Kingdom, which is a country.** Finally, a country! Its full name is the United Kingdom of Great Britain and Northern Ireland, but don't call it UKGBNI; the UK is fine. England, Scotland, and Wales are all semiautonomous, meaning that they have regional governments of varying kinds, but the national Parliament has the real power. London is the capital of both England and the United Kingdom.

The **British Isles comprise Great Britain, Ireland, and about five thousand nearby smaller islands** including the Channel Islands, the Isle of Man, and the Isle of Wight. Many of them are self-governing dependencies of the British crown rather than official parts of the United Kingdom.

Another distinction: Ireland is the name of the island consisting of Northern Ireland (again, part of the UK) and the Republic of Ireland (a sovereign country, called Eire if you're a local or a purist).

In sum, England is a political division. Great Britain is an island. The United Kingdom is a country. The British Isles are a geographic designation. So if you go to England, you're also in Great Britain, the United Kingdom, and the British Isles at the same time. But you'll get only one stamp in your passport.

RELATED TERM: *Sometimes the island of Great Britain is referred to as* **Britain,** *and sometimes the entire UK is nicknamed Britain.*

What's the difference between...
a HIGHWAY, a FREEWAY, an EXPRESSWAY, and a PARKWAY?

Highways aren't always high, freeways aren't always free, expressways aren't always express routes, and parkways are never parks. Now that we've gotten that out of the (high/free/express/park) way...

HIGHWAY

In the United States, *highway* is a **catchall term for a large high-speed road** (see page 139) designed for cars. Highways usually have multiple lanes in both directions, a median divider, and access ramps that are farther apart than connections on a standard road. They can meander through only one city or link more than one city.

FREEWAY

A freeway is a **multiple-lane highway with no cross traffic.** Freeways have controlled access at interchanges, or junctions where traffic can move from one highway to another without crossing streams of traffic. This is accomplished with overpasses and underpasses. Motorists enter and exit freeways via a limited number of on-ramps and off-ramps. Traffic flows in both directions (on either side of a barrier, thankfully). Freeways have no traffic lights, stop signs, crosswalks, speed bumps, or other obstacles to speed. Among all "-ways," "freeway" is most commonly used in the United States. Despite the name, many freeways have tollbooths. The "free" refers to the fact that traffic is supposed to flow freely.

At times and in certain parts of the country, some of these terms have slightly different meanings—or are used interchangeably, particularly "freeway" and "expressway."

EXPRESSWAY

An expressway is also a divided, **multiple-lane highway, but with limited access at grade intersections,** or points where the expressway crosses another road on the same level. Traffic can't reach property adjacent to the expressway directly, but can do so by using a frontage road, a local road that runs parallel to the expressway. Some expressways have traffic lights.

PARKWAY

A parkway is a **divided highway reserved only for passenger cars.** As its name suggests, it is a scenic route, specially lined with foliage, not billboards or other traces of the "sell, sell, sell" world. Even commercial traffic, such as trucks and buses, is often prohibited on parkways.

RELATED TERMS: *An* **interstate** *is a highway that is part of the federal network of major roads; despite the name, some interstates do not cross state (see page 68) lines.*

A **turnpike** *is a highway with tolls; the term turns up in various regions, not nationally.*

*"**Thruway**" is a synonym for expressway.*

What's the difference between...
the NETHERLANDS and HOLLAND?

One is the medieval name and the other the modern? Wrong. One is what it's called inside the country and the other internationally? Wrong. Both are part of its official name, "the Federated States of the Netherlands and the Territory of Holland"? Wrong (though inventive).

The Netherlands is a **country,** and Holland comprises but two of its twelve **provinces,** Noord-Holland and Zuid-Holland (North Holland and South Holland; Holland was divided this way in 1840). **Holland occupies the northwestern portion of the Netherlands.**

Don't feel pity if Holland is not as high up the hierarchy as you might have thought. Historically, much of the economic and cultural renown of the Netherlands has been split between the two provinces. That extends to the present: Noord-Holland contains Amsterdam, which is the capital of the Netherlands, and Zuid-Holland contains the Hague, which is the seat of government.

Netherlands means "low countries" and *Holland* means "wooded land." To English speakers, the people who live in the Netherlands, and by extension Holland, are the Dutch.

The only period when the name of the country that is now called the Netherlands referenced Holland was between 1806 and 1810, when it was called the Napoleonic Kingdom of Holland.

Despite the actuality, the names of some Dutch embassies (see page 130) indicate the country they represent as Holland rather than the Netherlands.

Paris, France / Paris, America

Paris is the capital of and largest city in France, which is in turn the largest member (in area) of the European Union. The population of Paris is more than 2.1 million. It's a cultural center not only of France but of Europe, and indeed the world.

At least twelve towns in America are also named Paris, not including those named New Paris, West Paris, This Here's Paris, and so on. Populations according to the 2000 U.S. Census:

Paris, Texas	25,898
Paris, Tennessee	9,763
Paris, Kentucky	9,183
Paris, Illinois	9,077
Paris, Maine	4,793
Paris, New York	4,609
Paris, Arkansas	3,707
Paris, Missouri	1,529
Paris (Kenosha County), Wisconsin	1,473
Paris (Grant County), Wisconsin	754
Paris, Idaho	576
Paris, Michigan	567

None of these towns is the cultural center of France, Europe, or indeed the world, and none appears to be a cultural center of the United States, either, though their hospitality is presumed to be warmer than a freshly baked casserole.

What's the difference between...
a ROAD, a STREET, a BOULEVARD, a LANE, and an AVENUE?

Different-colored lights on a traffic light. Different styles of lane dividers (dotted, solid, single, double, yellow, white). Different cyclist hand signals (meaning turn indicators, not rude gestures). There are so many details a driver needs to know to be safe…but the differences among these driving surface terms is not one of them.

To some people, many of these terms are simply synonyms. Although some insist that there are differences, there are also exceptions at every turn (kind of a pun but kind of based in fact, too). Plus, differences can depend on where in the country or world you're driving.

Some U.S. cities and counties base street and avenue names on the direction of flow. In Manhattan, east-west is a street, north-south is an avenue. In some areas, specific designations are reserved for particular types of roads, such as meandering, dead end, diagonal, private, and so on, but the public is usually not aware of this.

One way these terms are clearly differentiated is Associated Press style. When written as part of a numbered address, Street, Avenue, and Boulevard should be abbreviated St., Ave., and Blvd. All other designations—Road, Place, Drive, and so on—should be written out.

ROAD

Generally, a road is **any open way** on which vehicles or people travel.

STREET

A street is often a road in an **urban environment** that is wider than an alley and sandwiched by sidewalks and buildings. According to this usage, a street is more heavily traveled than a road.

BOULEVARD

A boulevard is commonly a **wide, long thoroughfare with attractive landscaping** on both sides, down the middle, or both. In some cases, boulevards have nondescript medians such as a slab of concrete. Some medians also include pedestrian walkways.

LANE

A lane is a **narrow, often bucolic path** that lacks a shoulder or median. In another sense, a lane is, of course, a division of a larger road. This is manifested in terms of both driving (passing lane) and parking (fire lane).

AVENUE

An avenue, alas, does not seem to follow enough of a pattern to have any distinction whatsoever, though avenues sometimes align with the **characteristics of a boulevard.**

RELATED TERMS: *Drive, place, court, circle, terrace, trail, extension, way, crescent… don't get us started.*

What's the difference?

ARTS AND LEISURE

HIP-HOP and RAP

KUNG FU, KARATE, and JUDO

MANGA and ANIME

QUOTE and QUOTATION

"STORY BY," "SCREENPLAY BY," and "WRITTEN BY"

What's the difference between...
HIP-HOP and RAP?

Since the 1980s, people have been shaking their booties and/or thangs without realizing what was setting up the beat. No shame in that. But here's a shout-out to the truth.

HIP-HOP

Hip-hop is a **culture** with roots among black and Latino youth, particularly in New York City in the 1970s. Its four central components are deejaying, graffiti, b-boying, and emceeing. Deejaying is sometimes written "DJing," graffiti is sometimes called tagging, b-boying is usually—but incorrectly—called breakdancing, and emceeing is sometimes written "MCing." However, the general public knows MCing as another word altogether—rapping.

As its popularity spread, hip-hop culture developed its own flavor of existing cultural categories such as fashion, slang, and political activism. Hip-hop music, which is not the same thing as rap, is sometimes defined as a fusion of rapping and deejaying. Sometimes the distinction seems to be that hip-hop music is driven by sung lyrics and a combination of instruments rather than spoken lyrics and a dominant beat.

RAP

Rap, a **style of music,** is one of the four components of hip-hop, a culture. Rap features spoken, rhyming lyrics accompanying a beat and sprinkled with sampling, scratching, and mixing. The Sugar Hill Gang is credited with the first mainstream rap hit, "Rapper's Delight," in 1979. Rap is often an element of

hip-hop music. Purists will clarify that not every song with rapping in it should be classified as rap music, or hip-hop for that matter, and that not all hip-hop music has rap in it. But if the groove grabs you, don't stop and worry about these nuances. Just obey it.

Bonus Track/Hidden Track

Everyone expects greatest hits albums to contain filler–songs that weren't really hits. Record labels rationalize that even if it's deceptive, nobody cares–diehard fans already love the filler and casual listeners won't bother to look up the history of each song.

Tricks are not just the province of greatest hits collections. Regular albums also regularly pull a trick, in one of two forms–the bonus track or the hidden track. Regardless of which format is used, such a track is usually wack.

A bonus track is indicated in the track listing and liner notes. You'll recognize which it is because it's almost always last, plus it's conveniently labeled "bonus track." Of course, *bonus* implies both something extra and something desirable (see page 166). The music business is glad the general public has not realized that neither is actually the case when it comes to many of these bonus tracks. Since there is no fixed number of songs for a music CD, how can something be extra? While a CD is in production, it's simple smoke and mirrors to knock a twelve-track set down to eleven tracks but upgrade the twelfth track to "bonus" status. The customer won't be informed that it started out as unmodified old track twelve. If a so-called bonus song *wasn't* on an album, we wouldn't get that vague feeling that we're being cheated. And if it was there but *not* called a bonus (hello again, unmodified track twelve), we wouldn't recognize that it's something (supposedly) special disguised as something standard.

A hidden track is not listed anywhere on the CD or its package. (Or *is* it...?) On the disc, it's also most commonly last. Sometimes it's a separate track; this is apparent if the printed material accompanying the CD lists, say, ten songs but your CD player shows eleven. Sometimes, to circumvent that giveaway clue, the hidden track is tacked onto the last listed song but cushioned by a stretch of silence beforehand–perhaps a minute, perhaps nine minutes and forty-one seconds, or perhaps some other arbitrary length of time. Artists maintain that hidden tracks are surprises for the listener, and that is true–but what nobody likes to talk about is that not all surprises are welcome. Yes, not all surprises are bonuses. Indelicate magazines, stolen money, forbidden love, tattoos obtained in drunken youth–we hide things that we don't want others to know about. Therefore, by calling these songs "hidden," artists are inadvertently warning us that they may clog our ears with aural manure.

What's the difference between...
KUNG FU, KARATE, and JUDO?

Most of us who don't socialize with ninjas or samurais have a hazy if not opaque understanding of these terms. All are systems of fighting grouped under the martial arts, and all have Asian heritage. Warriors trained in a martial art to be prepared for either armed or unarmed combat. The martial arts depend on an orchestrated network of moves. More recently, some martial arts have been adapted as sports.

KUNG FU

Kung fu has become a **generic term for all Chinese martial arts.** The term means "hard work" or "skilled achievement" and actually **can be applied to any accomplishment,** not just martial arts. Therefore, "kung fu shuffleboarding" and "kung fu yodeling" are entirely feasible usages. The form became widely known in the United States with the rise of so-called kung fu movies of the 1960s. Compared to some Japanese styles, Chinese martial arts in general are typified by more fluid motions and may resemble more of a performance than a method of fighting or defense. Monks began creating these techniques around 300 B.C.E.

KARATE

Karate is a **Japanese martial art that predates judo** by about two centuries but which began its march to the mainstream in the twentieth century. It was influenced by Chinese forms and features both defenses and attacks, with an emphasis on power. It means "empty hand" or "open hand." Among the jabbing motions associated with karate are kicks, chops, and punches. Throws and grappling are typically not part of karate. As with other martial arts, karate has a number of styles. It is considered a **"hard" martial art** (as opposed to "soft").

A Western oversimplification that may earn you a chop to the neck: karate is akin to boxing, judo is akin to wrestling, and kung fu incorporates elements of both.

JUDO

Judo is a **Japanese martial art** involving both defenses and attacks, particularly the tactic of temporarily yielding, only to spring a surprise counterattack. These tactics include throws, pins, blocks, grappling, and joint locks. Knowing how to flip an opponent of any size is an integral part of judo. In 1882, a man named Jigoro Kano founded judo specifically as a sport. It was added to the Olympics in 1964. It is considered a **"soft" martial art;** *judo* means "way of peace."

RELATED TERMS: Aikido *is a "soft" Japanese martial art, founded by Morihei Uyeshiba in 1942, that focuses exclusively on defense. It consists of circular movements including throws, pins, rolls, and blocks that redirect an attacker's energy. It is one of the gentler martial arts.*

Jujitsu *(sometimes jiu-jitsu or jujutsu) is a Japanese martial art similar to (and inspiration for) judo, except that it also includes more dangerous offensive moves. Samurais learned jujitsu.*

Tae kwon do *is a Korean martial art characterized by an assortment of high kicks. Besides judo, it's the only other martial art currently in the Olympics.*

What's the difference between...
MANGA and ANIME?

If you're the thrill-seeking type, stroll into a comic shop and ask an employee this question loud enough so the patrons can also hear. You'll get some rolled eyes, probably a few pitying groans, and possibly a disgusted comment or two. Someone will explain that one is Japanese comics and the other is animation. You can then earn immediate redemption by revealing that you were on a dare and proving it by rattling off any of the following details—all of which they'll already know.

MANGA

Manga, which means "whimsical pictures," are **Japanese comics** populated by vibrant characters with oversized eyes, spiked hair, nubs for noses, and exaggerated expressions.

The following for this distinctive art form is immense in Japan and has spread worldwide. Published in magazines featuring multiple series, manga is produced in prolific amounts. Some of these magazines run more than eight hundred pages. The Japanese hold manga in high esteem, as art but also as literature. It has permeated their culture to the point that people have opened—and many actually go to—manga cafés. The manga style is seemingly influenced by a cocktail of nineteenth-century Japanese ukiyo-e (paintings and woodblock prints) and Western pop culture. Arguably the first manga creation to make a name for himself was Osamu Tezuka's Astro Boy. The adventures of this young robot superhero debuted in 1952. Some U.S. publishers have been experimenting with manga interpretations of established characters, such as Sabrina the Teenage Witch.

Some Japanese use "manga" to refer to both comics and animation, and some still use the term "Japanimation" instead of "anime."

ANIME

Anime is **TV or film animation in the manga style.** *Anime* is the Japanese translation of the English word *animation*. Like manga, anime employs certain stylistic techniques, such as wide mouths and stress marks on foreheads. The wide-eyed look of the characters comes from Tezuka, who in turn based that feature on American characters such as Betty Boop and Bambi. At times, anime animators take shortcuts, particularly for television animation. For example, they'll show a still image of a character moving across a background instead of animating him. Anime creators developed genres such as "giant robots" and "magical girls."

Similar to successful American comic book series, many of the popular manga stories are adapted into filmed media. Astro Boy's first TV series launched in 1963. Among the others that have gone from page to screen—and have reached U.S. shores—are *Dragon Ball Z* and *Yu-Gi-Oh!* Even some longstanding American properties have been recast in anime or a variation of it, such as *Teen Titans*. An anime film, *Spirited Away* (2003), received the second Academy Award given for Best Animated Feature.

"May I quotation you on that?" To people who lived in the nineteenth century—and to certain sticklers today—that was and is just as incorrect as "What is your favorite quote about love?" Apologies for bringing grammar into this, but in formal circles, *quote* and *quotation* play for different teams.

QUOTE

Quote is a **verb** meaning "to repeat words of a person and attribute them accordingly." Here's an example: "My eighth-grade history teacher liked to quote Garfield—the cat, not the president."

Now *quote* is also **regularly used as a noun,** but not to irk anyone—people just don't realize the distinction. The acceptability of *quote* as a noun depends on the editor (because, really, who else cares?). In speech and informal writing, there's usually no quibble, but in formal writing, *quotation* is preferred. This is especially true when quoting figures who are not contemporary. With Thomas Jefferson, you'll want *quotation*. With David Letterman, feel free to go with *quote*.

"Never Forget"/"Always Remember" in Advertising

This is provided as a public service announcement and a swift elbow to the gut of certain Hollywood and Broadway copywriters. Enough with the "characters we'll always remember" in a "story we'll never forget"—and all other variations of those phrases. We know there's no difference between them. It makes us wonder how good could the movie or musical be if the promotion (see page 167) is so uninspired?

Quotation is a **noun** meaning "words of one person repeated by another." Here's an example: "People often start a speech with a quotation— it's easier to lean on someone else's cleverness than to show some of your own."

The word is **never used as a verb.** Exact wording is implied, though some print journalists would still use *quotation* to refer to a statement whose language but not meaning has been tweaked in editing (for example, deleting "uhs" and "ums," omitting false starts, substituting an unclear passage with more precise words or phrases in brackets, and so on). Others would say that if even one word is changed, it's no longer a quotation.

RELATED TERM: Quotation marks *are punctuation used to set off a quotation. It's double quotation marks for a regular quotation, single quotation marks for a quotation within a quotation. If you want to quote me on that, you'd write, "'Quotation marks are punctuation used to set off a quotation,' according to* What's the Difference?"

What's the difference between...
"STORY BY," "SCREENPLAY BY," and "WRITTEN BY"?

Hollywood filmmaking is a collaborative art that begins even before the first scene is shot. Even before the actors are hired. Yes, even before merchandising rights are sold. A screenwriter will tell you that, creditwise, he's probably going to be screwed in one of two ways. One, either his name will stay on a film he originated or wrote an early draft for although subsequent writers rewrote it so much (and often, so badly) that none of his work remains. Or, two, he'll be the rewrite guy who molds the screenplay into brilliance but who won't get credit due to one of the following policies, each of which carries its own formulas of just how much of a script a person needs to contribute (and when) to earn that particular credit.

"STORY BY"

A "story by" credit is given to the person or team who **came up with the essence of a film** (such as the plot or main characters) and who may have written a treatment **but didn't write the screenplay.** Similarly, a "screen story by" credit goes to a person or team who adapted other material such as a novel, a TV show, or a news article for film and made it substantially different from the source.

"SCREENPLAY BY"

A "screenplay by" credit is given to the person or team who **wrote** the scenes and dialogue of a screenplay **but didn't generate the idea for the story.**

"WRITTEN BY"

A "written by" credit is given to the person or team who both **conceived of the story and wrote the screenplay.** It usually merges "story by" and "screenplay by."

RELATED TERMS: "And" *indicates multiple writers or writing teams who contributed but did not collaborate directly—they may never have even met. Examples are "Andrew Douglas and Justin Goldstein" or "Mike Fox and Bethany Kant and Rachel Loonin."*

An **ampersand (&)** *indicates multiple people or teams who wrote together. Examples are "Darren Sapper & Matt Small" or "Kevin Alansky & Rachel Fremont and Seth Kessler & Dara Neumann." (Here, Alansky and Fremont wrote together, Kessler and Neumann wrote together, but the two pairs did not make it a foursome.) You might also see a team and an individual, such as "Mike Chasen & Randi Skylar and Chris Campagnuolo."*

What's the difference?

AROUND THE HOUSE

ALUMINUM FOIL SHINY SIDE and ALUMINUM FOIL DULL SIDE

ANTIQUE and COLLECTIBLE

CARPET and RUG

COUCH and SOFA

What's the difference between...
ALUMINUM FOIL SHINY SIDE and
ALUMINUM FOIL DULL SIDE?

Say goodbye to agonizing moments spent trying to decide which way to wrap a soon-to-be-baked potato. Aside from appearance, there is virtually no difference between shiny and dull sides of aluminum foil.

In manufacturing, two layers of aluminum foil are fed through rollers instead of one. This helps prevent tearing, since the material is so thin. The two outer sides—the ones in contact with the polished steel rollers—become reflective, while the two inner sides—facing each other—emerge with a matte finish.

Some claim that these sides can be used strategically in cooking. Since shiny surfaces reflect heat, they say wrap foods to be cooked with the shiny side facing inward, to bounce the heat back at the food and theoretically cook it faster. But in practice, this amounts to an **unnoticeable difference.** Though some specialty foils come with both sides shiny, there has yet to be a market push to offer all-shiny and all-dull foil as separate products. Stay tuned, though.

RELATED TERM: Tin foil *(sometimes tinfoil) is a product no longer in use, commercially replaced by aluminum foil in the 1920s. It was more rigid than aluminum foil and left food with a tinny taste. Aluminum foil today is almost all aluminum, and no foil contains tin. People hold on to the outdated term due to ignorance or nostalgia, or maybe just because it's a few less syllables.*

"I Like You as a Friend"/"It's Not You, It's Me"

To many of us, being turned down stings no matter what form it takes. Yet these two rejections—possibly the most widely employed in the dating scene—are not the same. Whether you are male or female, straight or gay, if you learn the nuances, you will be better prepared for a comeback that could swing things back in your favor.

Coming from a female, "I like you as a friend" does not mean "You've got a great personality but I'm not attracted to you." This is a misinterpretation that overlooks the fact that women generally don't value appearance as highly as men do. What this really means is "I'm going to keep your number in case I need help moving." See, even personality plays no part in it. Yet a man's best recourse here is to work on both his looks and his attitude in case she ever does call for a favor involving heavy-lifting—that would be your chance to win her back while straining yours.

When a female says "It's not you, it's me," men usually believe that she's reversing the "you" and "me" only to be polite. However, unlike the phrase examined above, the woman is telling the truth in this case. She is coming right out and saying, "I am crazy and am giving you fair warning." The smart man will take this as an opportunity to suggest therapy, winning her all over again by adding that he'll be supportive throughout the process.

These phrases have different meanings when males say them. "I like you as a friend" from a man means "I actually don't like you but if you want to sleep with me, I'm fine with that." Like the female equivalent, a male "It's not you, it's me" is also the truth. The translation is "It's not you (who has a problem with this—or any—relationship), it's me."

In either case, if the woman still likes the man at this point, she can say, "Well, that should free me up to spend more time with Tony," which will prompt a single-minded man to issue an immediate retraction. If not, she can tweak it as follows: "Well, that should free me up to spend more time with Tony, Sven, and Carlos." Sometimes it takes three men to do the job of one.

What's the difference between...
an ANTIQUE and a COLLECTIBLE?

Nothing is created to be an antique and anything created can be a collectible (sometimes spelled "collectable"). Well, these days, some people *do* create products meant to look old and pass them off as antiques, but their unscrupulousness doesn't derail the distinction.

ANTIQUE

An antique is an item **at least one hundred years old,** particularly one that falls into the subjective categories of beautiful, rare, or unique. Therefore, every year a new batch of things is quietly inducted into the "antique hall of fame."

It's not just age that determines which antiques are valuable; as with most everything else, demand also plays a role. By definition, antiques are items resold after their initial distribution and sale, meaning that they're in the secondary market (sounds less scruffy than "used"). Before U.S. tax law set the hundred-year threshold, an item was called an antique if it was made before 1820 or 1830. And despite that tax law, some dealers today will label items as young as fifty years an antique. In fashion, "antique" applies to clothes through the 1920s. With cars, it applies to those twenty-five years old or older. In both of those cases and certain others, many antiques are no longer viable or desirable for everyday use.

RELATED TERMS: Vintage *summons a certain past era, which varies depending on the product. Vintage clothing currently includes items from the 1930s to the 1970s and even, in some cases, the 1980s. Some say that vintage clothes are not just any clothes from that period (as one might find at a thrift shop), but only those in good condition and with a certain timeless style. Vintage automobiles are those produced between and including 1919 and 1930, though some definitions end at 1925 while others extend to the start of World War II. With various other items less than a hundred years old, the phrase* **"vintage collectible"** *is sometimes used.*

COLLECTIBLE

A collectible is any item that someone, somewhere, for reasons judged sound or silly, collects. This can include antiques, but it also can include swim goggles or lozenge wrappers manufactured last week.

The collectibles market is more trend-driven than the antiques market. Commonly, the term indicates something **contemporary and mass-produced** for the express purpose of being collected—Beanie Babies, for example. Some antiques dealers regard collectibles with contempt, but the fact remains that many, many people don't. (Visit eBay for proof.) Most antiques are collectibles, but the reverse is not always true.

Retro *is a largely design-related term that usually refers to clothes and home décor of the 1960s and 1970s. At times, it is used to indicate the look as well as the actual output of that period, meaning that newly produced clothes representing past styles count as retro, too.*

What's the difference between...
a CARPET and a RUG?

Carpets may seem so rec room and rugs so palace, but there isn't really a vast chasm between the two.

CARPET	RUG
A carpet is **typically bigger** than a rug.	A rug is typically described as a weave that is of a certain size or smaller. Some sources claim that size is four feet by six feet (1.2 m by 1.8 m), while others say it's forty square feet (3.7 sq m).
It's almost always found **on the floor.**	Either way, a rug seems to be regarded as slightly more versatile than a carpet. Of course, a rug is commonly used as a floor decoration, but you can also **hang a rug on the wall, lay it across a bed, or nestle it around the hearth.** It can even be placed over a carpet to liven up the décor.
Within the world of floor coverings, a distinction is also made between carpet and carpeting. The latter is wall-to-wall and laid down in strips over a cushion to form a continuous plush surface. In real estate lingo, a carpet is usually distinguished from a rug in that it's **attached to the floor.**	A realtor would define a rug as loose, **not fixed to the floor** in some way. Some rug dealers may define a rug as a floor covering that can be made out of any material, from fabric to animal hide. Others may describe it as an unfinished weave fresh from the loom, as opposed to a carpet, which is a product complete with fringes or smoothed edges.

What's the difference between...
a COUCH and a SOFA?

Are you sitting down for this one? If so, on what? If you said couch, you might have been able to get away with sofa, and vice versa.

COUCH

A couch is a piece of furniture on which at least two people can comfortably sit or at least one can recline. The word is frequently used interchangeably with "sofa." However, when it comes to what you lie on during therapy sessions, you think "couch." The term has also inherited a reputation for being an **enabler of laziness.** After all, you never hear of a "sofa potato."

SOFA

A sofa is, well, see "couch." Often, a sofa has arms and a back and is usually upholstered (but then again, same with couches). While sofas are designed for sitting, some also convert into sleeping units called sofa beds (since "sleeping unit" is too clinical). The most common distinction from a couch—which may actually be a misconception—is that a sofa is **somehow fancier.** If anything, a couch may be, at least historically. When you think of a finely crafted (though stiff-looking) eighteenth-century piece of furniture with a back that curves sensuously up to a headrest, you're thinking of what was typically called a couch, not a sofa. Today, some sofas are sold as part of a set that includes a matching chair or two. They also may have "special features." And there's nothing pretentious about a built-in beer can holder.

What's the difference?

BUSINESS

COPYRIGHT and TRADEMARK

DEBIT CARD AS DEBIT CARD and DEBIT CARD AS CREDIT CARD

MARKETING and PROMOTION

What's the difference between...
a COPYRIGHT and a TRADEMARK?

Few commonly confused pairs spell out their differences in their names as clearly as copyright and trademark do. In short, a copyright is the *right* to *copy* your own work, while a trademark is a *mark* indicating the source of a good that is *traded.* Copyrights promote the arts while trademarks safeguard the reputations of companies.

COPYRIGHT

A copyright **protects original artistic, literary, dramatic, musical, and intellectual work that is fixed in any tangible medium,** such as a book, song, or computer program. The work can be published or unpublished. You can't copyright an idea. What you can copyright is the unique expression of an idea.

A copyright entitles the holder the exclusive right to reproduce, publicly distribute copies of, create derivative works of, publicly perform, and publicly display a work. These five rights kick in from the moment the work is written, illustrated, or constructed, even without registering. You don't even need to plaster a "copyright © 2006 My Name" on your as-yet-unpublished Great American Novel or nude sculpture of yourself, though that may deter potential thieves. However, you're safest if you do officially register your work.

Copyrights are registered with the **U.S. Copyright Office** and are generally easier to register than trademarks. A copyright registration currently costs $30 and takes approximately four to five months to process.

A copyright remains in effect for **seventy years after the creator's death,** and no renewal is necessary; and, unlike with a trademark, the holder is under no pressure to keep tabs on it constantly.

Copyright law is fairly consistent from country to country.

TRADEMARK

A trademark **protects words, names, titles, symbols, logos, and designs that are used to identify the source of a good.**

Once you slap the trademark symbol on a product in public commerce, it's legitimate—though as with copyrights, it's to your advantage to register from the get-go. Trademarks help companies maintain a distinctive identity in the marketplace. However, they don't prevent other companies from producing the same goods imprinted with a clearly different mark. That is to say that, also like copyrights, you can't trademark an idea.

Trademarks are registered with the **U.S. Patent and Trademark Office.** A trademark registration currently costs $325 to $375 and often takes a year or up to several years to process, since there is more research involved in issuing it.

Trademarks protect, but they must also be protected. Companies monitor their trademarks so that they don't slip into generic use; if they do, they can lose them. Kleenex wants the public to know that *Kleenex* is the specific brand of one company, not a universal synonym for *tissue*. A trademark **must be renewed every ten years.**

Trademark law can vary significantly among different countries.

a DEBIT CARD AS DEBIT CARD and
a DEBIT CARD AS CREDIT CARD?

Note the distinction within this difference: it's not a comparison between debit and credit cards but rather the two forms of use of debit cards—PIN-based (ATM card style) and signature-based (credit card style). If they are emblazoned with the logo of a major credit card company, debit cards can be used either way. The decision affects consumer and retailer.

DEBIT CARD AS DEBIT CARD

Debit as debit requires a customer to **punch in his PIN. This withdraws funds from his checking account immediately,** akin to paying with cash. Debit cards are sometimes called check cards, though they suck the money from an account faster than a check does. In debit as debit purchases, the **merchant pays a flat fee per transaction,** regardless of the amount, so this way is usually a better deal for him. Consumers also have the option to get **cash back** from participating merchants, in effect treating the store like an ATM machine. Some banks charge debit as debit users a monthly fee or a fee per transaction, as if they're using a foreign ATM. Consumers don't need to flash a photo ID when using debit as debit.

DEBIT CARD AS CREDIT CARD

Debit as credit requires a customer to **sign the receipt.** He punches in "credit" rather than "debit" on the checkout keypad, but it's not a true credit situation. As with debit as debit, the **funds are withdrawn from the customer's checking account, but not right away;** it usually happens within two to three days. In debit as credit purchases, the **merchant's fee is a percentage of the amount of the sale,** say 1.5 percent. Consumers **aren't able to get cash back this way.** In some cases, they'll have to show photo ID when using debit as credit.

RELATED TERMS: *What about debit as credit card versus a straight-up* **credit card?** *Whether you go PIN or pen with a debit card, it's still a gateway to your account. That's why financial folks encourage limiting all debit card use to smaller, in-person purchases—anywhere you'd just as well use cash. And don't let debit cards out of your sight. Credit cards provide the consumer with a higher level of protection against fraud. Use them instead of debit cards when making large purchases or when shopping online. That way, it will be easier for you to get refunds or replacements for items damaged in shipment or items that never arrive.*

Within the debit as debit difference is yet another difference—debit card versus **ATM card.** *An ATM card is solely for getting cash at an ATM machine and is not programmed for use as a debit card. Bare-bones ATM cards don't have Visa or MasterCard logos.*

What's the difference between...
MARKETING and PROMOTION?

A good marketer for this very book would seek out comparable titles and find out who bought them, then devise clever ways to appeal to that group. (On that note, recommend this book to your relatives, friends, colleagues! Also, it makes a great gift!) A good promoter might devise clever ways to appeal to certain people, but might not spend time figuring out who those people are.

MARKETING

Marketing is a process in which you **determine and analyze potential buyers** for a product or service, then **capture their attention,** then **persuade them to take action**—in other words, persuade them to drop that "potential" before "buyer" and subsequently drop money into your coffers. Marketing is an ongoing strategy to reach and intrigue the customer, whether he is an existing customer or a new one. Most companies want to retain existing customers and attract new ones at the same time. The end result of marketing is to make money by shrewdly targeting people who want what you're selling—and not waste resources on people who don't. Marketing can exist without promotion, though it doesn't make sense to develop a product or service and then sit back to see if the public finds it without any nudge from you.

PROMOTION

Promotion is **one of the four facets of marketing.** The other three facets are product (namely, how does it serve a need or fulfill a desire?), price, and distribution. Promotion can involve advertising, publicity, sales promotion, and personal selling—it's **the way a company sends its message to the public.** While promotion is designed to fatten profits, it can have other missions, too: to define a company's philosophy, to reinforce the image a company wants to portray, to demonstrate how a company is superior to a competitor, or to modestly show a different side of a company, such as its dedication to a charitable cause. Promotion can—and often does—exist without marketing, but some of it can fall on disinterested eyes and ears if no one has done the research required to focus promotions on the most receptive audience.

What's the difference?

HARD SURFACES

APRON and TARMAC

CEMENT and CONCRETE

PAVEMENT and ASPHALT

What's the difference between...
an APRON and TARMAC?

The amount of time we spend waiting in airports may be in reverse proportion to the amount of information we know about them—a lot versus a little. Chances are, you're about to be humbled for all those times you thought you sounded like a seasoned aviator by pointing through the huge lounge windows and referring to the "tarmac."

APRON

The apron is the large **concrete area at an airport** on which aircraft do all their slow-motion activities: taxi, park, refuel, load, and unload passengers. In the military, the apron is also known as the ramp.

TARMAC

Tarmac is a **material that has been used to create aprons,** among other surfaces. Similar to asphalt (see page 172) and short for the fabulously rhythmic "tar-penetration macadam," tarmac is composed of tar and pieces of stone. Created in the early 1900s to reduce dust on roadways, tarmac has since been replaced by paving materials that are easier to work with. Some people incorrectly believe that *tarmac* refers only to the paved area that is closest to airport terminals, but that is just as much a part of the apron as the rest of the asphalt desert that stretches into the distance.

What's the difference between...
CEMENT and CONCRETE?

This hard question has an easy answer.

CEMENT

Cement is a material made predominantly from **limestone, calcium, silicon, iron, and aluminum,** plus traces of other ingredients. When this mixture is heated to about 2,700 degrees Fahrenheit (1,482 degrees C), it transforms into a substance that resembles marbles. No kids play with them—they're ground to a powder and combined with gypsum to form cement. Water is added to bring about the hardening (not drying) process. Cement is properly called Portland cement, which is a generic term, not a brand name. We average people have actually never seen cement. Rather, we've seen what it helps constitute: concrete.

CONCRETE

Concrete is **cement plus sand and gravel.** When in pastelike form, cement binds the crushed rock into the skull-cracking surface we know concrete to be. You can liken the relationship between cement and concrete to flour and bread, which is not to say you want your bread to be as hard as concrete. Cement makes up 10 to 15 percent of the mass of concrete. Though concrete is strong, there are times when it needs to be even stronger, such as in bridges and skyscrapers. In those cases, it can be reinforced by being poured over steel rods and cables and being left to solidify. In construction, concrete is used more frequently than any other material of its kind. Luckily, the materials needed to create concrete (and cement) are abundant and the production of concrete and cement doesn't result in harmful byproducts.

Pavement is a hard surface of which asphalt is one type. Concrete is another. If you've already read the entry on concrete (see page 171), perhaps you've realized that a more apt comparison than pavement and asphalt is asphalt and concrete. (If not, then your head may be filled with one or both.)

Asphalt is a **viscous liquid** that is a natural part of most crude petroleum. It's sometimes mistaken for tar, which is an artificial substance.

Asphalt and concrete are the most common paving methods. (Making matters slightly confusing: *asphalt* is actually an abbreviation for the term "asphalt concrete.") Asphalt pavement is **flexible.** Concrete pavement is **rigid.** The key way in which this difference matters is weight distribution.

Asphalt pavement is weaker than concrete pavement and does not spread weight (be it automotive or foot traffic) as well. It also requires additional support, so usually one or more thick layers of gravel and stone are laid down over the compacted soil before the surface asphalt is applied. Because **asphalt is less expensive than concrete,** easier to use and maintain, and often quieter, more than 90 percent of the paved roads (see page 139) in the United States are made from asphalt.

The inherent stiffness of concrete pavement causes the load to be distributed over a wider area. Concrete pavement does not need as much material between it and the soil. In addition to being stronger than asphalt, **concrete is more enduring,** generally lasting twice as long before needing repair. In fact, it gets stronger as it gets older. Yet concrete rehabilitation is more expensive.

INDEX